"I found this book to be a real Point of Light as Dolphus shows us that things can change in this America. His inspirational and provocative story shows love over hate, reconciliation over opposition." —**Allen A. Belton**, Senior Partner, Reconciliation Ministries, Breakthrough Partners

"We hear much these days about the wisdom of staying put and serving in one place. This book shows how God gave Dolphus Weary a deep love for rural Mississippians and an abiding call to work for their redemption [through] some remarkable, gospel-driven community ministries [that] are deeply rooted in Mississippi but provide a model for ministry in impoverished communities nationwide. Along the way, Dolphus shares much wisdom on racial reconciliation, Christians' public witness in America, and interracial partnerships in ministry. This is a wonderful book, by a great storyteller and wise leader. Do read it, and better yet, take it to heart."
—**Joel Carpenter**, Director, Nagel Institute, Calvin College, and author of *Revive Us Again: The Reawakening of American Fundamentalism*

"Dolphus Weary shares the God-given wisdom he has received as he journeyed out of physical, emotional, and spiritual poverty. This book is a must-read for all followers of Jesus Christ who want to know God's heart for our broken world."
—**Dr. Peter Menconi**, author of *The Intergenerational Church*

"From The Mendenhall Ministries, to Mission Mississippi, and now through the R.E.A.L. Foundation, Dolphus and Rosie Weary have lived their lives to bring God's love to some of 'the least of these.' *Crossing the Tracks* is a personal story of commitment, as well as a practical guide to involvement, for those concerned about racial reconciliation and a calling to serve the poor. Buy it; read it; pass it on."
—**Phil Reed**, President/CEO, Voice of Calvary Ministries, Jackson, Mississippi

"I count Dolphus as a close adviser on many subjects, including race relations. You need to invest some time in reading this book; your life will be richer for it."
—**Scott Dawson**, Scott Dawson Evangelistic Association

"After reading this book you will feel . . . a need to reach out to the disadvantaged and share God's love with those who may not look like you."
—**Cheryl Sanford-Givens**, former board member of Mission Mississippi

"Dolphus Weary tackles the tough issues of racial reconciliation with a winsome, easy way that makes you think you are having a friendly, honest conversation on your front porch." —**Rick Langeloh**, Executive Pastor, Menlo Park Presbyterian Church

"Dolphus Weary, out of a lifetime of personal experience, speaks on race relations in clear, insightful, and thought-provoking terms, which will challenge your sensitivity to racial issues." —**Ken Nielsen**, former chair, InterVarsity Christian Fellowship

"A pertinent page-turner. . . . The honesty, life experience, information, and insights presented in this book will encourage those who are trying to hear and follow the Lord. It will make us more aware of and sensitive to the contemporary issues of poverty and racial discrimination. BRAVO Dolphus!"
—**Lynn Kolowsky**, InterVarsity Christian Fellowship board member

Crossing the Tracks

Hope for the Hopeless and Help for the Poor
in Rural Mississippi and Your Community

Dolphus Weary

with Josh Dear and William D. Hendricks

Kregel
Publications

Crossing the Tracks: Hope for the Hopeless and Help for the Poor in Rural Mississippi and Your Community
© 2012 by R.E.A.L. Christian Foundation

Published by Kregel Publications, a division of Kregel, Inc., P.O. Box 2607, Grand Rapids, MI 49501.

Library of Congress Cataloging-in-Publication Data
Weary, Dolphus, 1946-
Crossing the tracks : hope for the hopeless and help for the poor in rural Mississippi and your community / Dolphus Weary with Josh Dear and William D. Hendricks.
   p.   cm.
1. Race relations—Religious aspects—Christianity. 2. Mississippi—Race relations. 3. Church work with the poor—Mississippi. 4. Community development—Mississippi. 5. Weary, Dolphus, 1946– 6. Mendenhall Ministries (Mendenhall, Miss.) I. Dear, Josh. II. Hendricks, William, 1954– III. Title.
BT734.2.W43   2012   277.62'083—dc23   2012010776

ISBN 978-0-8254-4169-1

Printed in the United States of America
12 13 14 15 16 / 5 4 3 2 1

To my wife, Rosie Camper Weary,
my son, Ryan D. Weary,
my daughter, Dr. Danita R. Weary,
my grandson, Lil Reggie, and
the staff of R.E.A.L. Christian Foundation

Contents

Foreword by Neddie Winters   9

Acknowledgments   13

1   "Thank You, Mr. President!"   15

2   "I Ain't Comin' Back!" (But I Did)   21

3   Miracles in Mendenhall   30

4   "I Can't Never Leave!"   49

5   The Sin of Silence   65

6   The Power of Parenting   87

7   A Level Playing Field   117

8   Building Bridges of Reconciliation   137

9   "Thank You, America!"   167

10   Making It R.E.A.L.   174

Afterword: The 300 Club   189

Foreword

When I met Dolphus Weary more than two decades ago, little did I know the impact he would have on my life and the lives of so many others. As I reflect on my relationship with Dolphus, I am reminded of the biblical passage in Hebrews 12:1–3.

> Therefore, since we are surrounded by such a huge crowd of witnesses to the life of faith, let us strip off every weight that slows us down, especially the sin that so easily hinders our progress. And let us run with endurance the race that God has set before us. We do this by keeping our eyes on Jesus, on whom our faith depends from start to finish. He was willing to die a shameful death on the cross because of the joy he knew would be his afterward. Now he is seated in the place of highest honor beside God's throne in heaven. Think about all he endured when sinful people did such terrible things to him, so that you don't become weary and give up. (NLT)

I heard about Dolphus and his book *I Ain't Comin' Back* several years before I met him, with many people encouraging me to hear him and read his book. Well, I heard Dolphus speak, purchased his book, and even had him speak at my church, though I did not immediately read the book. I was convinced that all black people growing up in Mississippi had this dream of leaving and never coming back. I didn't need to read his book or any other book to understand the pain of poverty, racism, and discrimination. I had experienced it all. But I finally did read the book, and it gave me a greater understanding of racism and discrimination. The book also reinforced for me and gave greater resolve to my commitment to racial reconciliation and healing, as well as my commitment to help eradicate poverty in Mississippi.

I began working very closely with Dolphus in the early 1990s through The Mendenhall Ministry (TMM) with the Pastors Development Program, providing training and support to rural bi-vocational pastors. In addition to that work, we have been working together with Mission Mississippi for the past thirteen years to encourage and demonstrate unity in the body of Christ across racial and denominational lines so communities throughout Mississippi can better understand the gospel message.

Reading and understanding what Dolphus has experienced and sacrificed and seeing his continued passion and dedication to eliminate poverty, racism, and discrimination made me say wow! What an enrichment and encouragement for me, thus Hebrews 12:1–3.

It doesn't end here. Dolphus has written a new book entitled *Crossing the Tracks: Hope for the Hopeless and Help for the Poor in Rural Mississippi and Your Community.* At least that's what he is calling it. I call it *The Rest of the Story!* The reason for telling the rest of the story is because of the continuing work that Dolphus returned to Mississippi to do and how it is impacting his life, his family, and the greater community not only in Simpson County, Mississippi, but throughout the state, the nation, and the world.

Dolphus moves us forward in the right direction as only Dolphus can do in his *passionate* and *compassionate* way while dealing with some of the most controversial topics, including racial reconciliation, affirmative action, the sin of silence, and leveling the playing field. He challenges us to become bridge builders, better parents and grandparents, and to give more and do more individually right where we are. He does a wonderful job of not only encouraging us to celebrate all the miracles and accomplishments that God has done to overcome poverty, racism, and discrimination; he also helps us with the *why* and *how* of celebrating.

Again, it doesn't stop here—Dolphus gives us some of the "how tos" of moving forward with strategies and practical applications that work.

Both of Dolphus's books have really inspired me, motivated me, and challenged me, as well as enhanced and enriched my life, my family's lives, and the lives of so many others.

But the greater blessing for me has been the opportunity of working with Dolphus, growing with him, and having him as a friend and mentor. By now you probably have figured out that Dolphus Weary is my hero! Now my challenge to you is to read the book, get the vision, and go do the rest of the work and become someone's hero today.

NEDDIE WINTERS
President, Mission Mississippi
Pastor, Voice of Calvary Fellowship Church

Acknowledgments

My mother, Lucille Granderson, was married three times—one of which was to my father, Albert Weary—and out of the marriages she mothered ten children. I owe a lot to her.

My siblings have inspired me as well. Elgia Weary Clayton was the first to go to college, and she taught school for forty years. Melvin Weary was the smartest in our family and gave so much to all of us. Kathy Weary Large was the first to receive a PhD. Patricia Weary Holloway got married out of high school, went on to college after having two children and got her master's degree, and has taught school for many years since. Virgie Craft Harris chose not to go to college but devoted her life to her five children. Billy Craft received his degree in accounting and became the finance director for our work in Mendenhall. All of my family have had a major impact on my journey.

Rosie, after forty years of marriage, is still a major encourager and driver for me. Then there's our children: Dr. Danita Weary, our daughter who constantly gives me reason to smile; Reggie, our oldest son who went home to be with the Lord in 2004; Ryan, our baby son who's the gifted one in our family and is working to determine how God wants him to use his gifts; and last but not the least, our grandson, Reginald Malik, who keeps us young.

During the early days of this book's development, Tina McKinnis Womack gave countless hours to shape some of my original thoughts. Then Josh Dear became the one who worked with me in shaping the original manuscript. He interviewed a number of people, including Joseph Martin, Rick Cannada, Jarvis Ward, Charlotte Graham, Henry Joseph, Ron Potter, Thomas Jenkins, Gary Maze, Luder Whitlock, Roger Parrott, Elizabeth Perkins, Phil Reed, and Leslie Gipson.

Lee Paris has been a consistent friend and encourager, and Jasper Bacon, one who has followed my example, has been a friend as well. Bishop Ronnie Crudup is a growing leader in our state as a pastor and Christian leader. Victor Smith, John Perkins, and William Winter have been invaluable pioneers for me on my faith journey. Artis Fletcher and Neddie Winters have been my pastors who have engaged my life.

Those who have worked with me at R.E.A.L. Christian Foundation and Mission Mississippi have been great encouragers: Jon Elder, Virginia Chase, Linda Jackson, Otilia Sebuktekin, Cindy Cheeks, Richard Riley, Jennifer Lyles, Crystal Cline Jackson, Renata Scott, the late Charles Dunn, Grace Murrey, David Arnold, and Janet Thomas. And Dan Hall has taught me to see things from the perspective of a white Christian.

Thanks also to the family of my supporters, Vera Perkins, Hazel Hall, Gregg Chase, Marcia Reed, Jacqueline Crudup, Lisa Paris, and Tommie Winters.

And special thanks to Bill Hendricks, who shaped our final manuscript, and the Board of R.E.A.L Christian Foundation, who allow Rosie and me to keep dreaming.

CHAPTER 1

"Thank You, Mr. President!"

One of the greatest honors any citizen of the United States can ever receive is an invitation to meet the president at the White House in Washington, DC. That level of recognition is exclusively reserved for historic heroes and world-class champions.

But in December 1991, it was not I going to Washington to meet the president. It was the president of the United States coming to Mississippi to meet me.

Me! What an amazing thought: "The president wants to meet *me! Wow!*" But it was also a stunning thought: "Me? Why me? What have I done to merit this? How could this possibly be happening to me?"

And so, as my wife, Rosie, and I stood on the tarmac at Naval Air Station (NAS) Meridian, waiting for *Air Force One*, my mind kept pondering over and over: "What in the world am I doing here?"

The simple answer was that The Mendenhall Ministries (TMM)—the organization I had been a part of building for more than twenty years to address the needs of the poor in rural Mendenhall, Mississippi—was being honored with a Point of Light Award by President George H. W. Bush.

When President Bush came into office in 1988, he wanted to move people away from the idea that the government should be the answer to every problem. He believed that all too often Americans respond to their needs by saying, "The government should take care of that." Instead, he wanted people to start taking responsibility themselves for what was going on (or not going on) in their local communities. He especially wanted them to get behind any efforts—whether Christian or not—that were already making a significant difference in the social sector, and yet doing so without the assistance of government funding.

To give leadership to that initiative, Mr. Bush established the Thousand Points of Light campaign. The idea was to single out worthy individuals and organizations for presidential recognition as a Daily Point of Light.

To that end the White House solicited representatives from every state to recommend local groups that deserved to be considered for the Points of Light list. Then members of the president's administrative team fanned out across the country to follow up on those recommendations and narrow down the candidates to people and groups who were doing truly noteworthy things to improve their communities—again, with no government funding. The president would then look over the finalists and decide who should be named as a Point of Light.

As the president's program was getting underway, I was serving on the board of the Voice of Hope Ministries (VOH) in Dallas, Texas. Kathy and Sayers Dudley had founded VOH in 1981, based on the model we had developed at TMM. While their work differed from ours in that they were focused on the urban poor, the core needs were the same: education, leadership development, health care, legal services, overcoming racial and ethnic prejudices, opportunities for employment, and economic development.

The Dudleys and their team had worked tirelessly and innovatively to address those kinds of needs in a bold, intentional effort to break the cycle of poverty in the West Dallas community. All in the name of Christ and the gospel. All without a dime of government assistance.

Needless to say, VOH was exactly the kind of organization President Bush had in mind when he launched his campaign. So in 1991, VOH was designated as the 321st Point of Light.

The same thing had already happened for Lawndale Community Church in Lawndale, Illinois. Way back in 1982, Wayne Gordon, a young white pastor from the all-black Lawndale neighborhood of Chicago, had come down to Mendenhall and asked us a thousand questions about how he and his church might launch a holistic ministry to meet the needs of the poor.

Wayne's concern was whether a white person could be effective ministering to blacks. My concern was whether he and his team would stay the course long enough to see their effectiveness.

So I spoke to both of our concerns by telling him, "If you're willing to commit yourself to a long-term ministry and to live in the neighborhood, I don't think you'll have any problem."

That's exactly what Wayne did. He and his family became vital members of the Lawndale community, and everyone began to identify which needs to address first. In their case, a health clinic became a priority, and in time they opened one. Later came a thrift store and a recreation center.

To support their efforts, I began making regular visits to

Lawndale, and eventually joined their board. As with our own work in Mendenhall and the Dudleys' work in West Dallas, I saw firsthand what can happen when people's commitment to the gospel results in a commitment to community transformation. It was no surprise at all, then, that Lawndale had been named a Point of Light winner in 1989.

With VOH and Lawndale having received Point of Light Awards, I suppose it was only a matter of time before a couple of people decided to nominate TMM for recognition as well. Mississippi governor Ray Mabus signed the recommendation letter, which was itself a profound honor. Then in October 1991, I received a letter, followed by a phone call from the president's office, designating TMM as the 541st Point of Light. An official certificate to that effect, signed by the president, arrived shortly thereafter.

And so on the appointed day in 1991, Rosie and I drove from Mendenhall, which is south of Jackson, to NAS Meridian about two hours northeast to wait for the president to arrive for the Points of Light ceremony. Altogether, six organizations were being honored that day from the state of Mississippi.

When *Air Force One* landed, we had the great privilege of meeting the president and hearing his public commendation of our efforts. It was immensely gratifying, yet humbling, to know that out of all of the countless things that churches, nonprofits, community organizations, and dedicated individuals were doing to better our world, TMM had been tapped as one of those "thousand points of light."

So that's what happened. But that story alone does not fully answer the question, why was a sitting president coming to visit me? You see, I was about the last person on earth you would have ever predicted to end up being honored by a president.

The fact is, I grew up as a nobody in rural Mississippi. Or maybe I just wished I'd been a nobody, because then I might have been better off. The reality was, I was a black kid growing up in Mississippi in the late 1940s, '50s, and early '60s. If you know anything about the Deep South at that time, you know that growing up as a black kid in Mississippi was nothing short of a life-and-death matter. If poverty, hunger, and disease didn't kill you, racism, bigotry, or the Klan just might. I know, because it had already happened that way for my family: when my grandmother was a young lady, a man who was courting her was grabbed one night when he got off the train and was lynched. That was just one of more than five hundred documented lynchings in Mississippi before 1954.

You can read more about my childhood in my first book, *I Ain't Comin' Back*. You'll learn that I was one of eight children. That my father left the family when I was four. That my mother was a strong woman with strong character and was the bedrock of our family. That for a while we lived in a three-room "shotgun" house in D'Lo, Mississippi, that had no running water, plumbing, or electricity. That I began picking cotton almost from the time I could walk. That Mama treated our childhood aches and pains with home remedies like corn-shuck tea, spider webs, and turpentine. That Mama insisted we do our best at what little schooling we got. That we worked hard, and although we weren't expected to become much of anything, we would at least become the best we could be.

Mama kept us alive despite some very long odds. But not even the determination of a loving mother could overcome a system that was fundamentally stacked against us. By the time I was an adolescent, my mind-set had become firmly fixed: *No matter what I do, no matter how hard I work, I'll always be second-class here. The system is rigged against me, and I'll always make just enough to get by but never enough to get ahead. That's the way it is here, and it's never going to change!*

Of that I was quite certain: *it's never going to change!* So certain was I that I hatched a plan, a strategy, a dream. I was going to escape! I was going to get away from Mississippi! I talked about it with my brothers and sisters while we'd be chopping cotton. I lay awake at night thinking about it. I held onto that vision in my heart as a flickering source of hope in what seemed like a hopeless situation. Someday I would find a way to leave Mississippi. I didn't know exactly how I would get out. But I swore, "Someday I will! And when I do—I ain't never comin' back!"

That's not exactly the outlook you'd encourage a young man to have if he aspires to win a Point of Light Award. But I wasn't thinking about winning any awards when I was a boy. I was just looking for a way to survive. My ticket across the state line proved to be basketball. Not that I had NBA talent. But I didn't need to. All it took was a basketball scholarship to a small college in Los Angeles, and I was free. Free at last!

CHAPTER 2

"I Ain't Comin' Back!" (But I Did)

The man who opened the door to California for me was John Perkins. Reverend John Perkins was the most unusual minister I had ever met. Unlike so many preachers I was familiar with while growing up, he didn't go around wearing expensive suits, riding around in a Cadillac, or dining on the finest food a poor family could manage while their kids sat outside going hungry. He didn't even want people to call him Reverend Perkins. Just John.

What made John especially attractive to me, however, was that he had grown up in rural Mississippi almost the same way I had, in a family of sharecroppers. Sharecropping, also known as farming on halves, involved a black tenant farmer being allowed to farm the land of a white landowner. The landowner supplied the seed and fertilizer, and the black farmer supplied the labor. In principle, the harvest was to be split fifty-fifty between landowner and tenant farmer. But the tenant farmer's share was paid only after the landowner used it to settle any debts the tenant had incurred. Given the fact that many blacks were unable to do basic arithmetic (and many couldn't read, either), sharecropping was almost guaranteed to be an unjust system. Many a black family fell hopelessly into debt thanks to that way of farming, and it virtually doomed them to a lifetime of servitude. Sharecropping may have been one step up from slavery, but not by much.

That was John's life growing up. But on top of that, John personally experienced the worst of the blatant racism that existed in the Deep South in the 1930s and '40s when his brother Clyde was shot and killed by a police officer in New Hebron, Mississippi. "He didn't know his place," was the justification given.

The incident touched off enormous rage in John, who was never one to back down from a challenge. Finally, his family implored him to leave Mississippi, lest his anger get him into trouble—or get him killed.

John moved to Southern California. And despite having dropped out of school in the third grade, he began to thrive. He got a good job, began moving up in his company, and made enough money to buy a thirteen-room house. Not bad for a former sharecropper!

So what in the world put it into John Perkins's mind to move his family back to Mississippi in 1960—and to Mendenhall, of all places? The answer is that in California, John was confronted with the gospel of Jesus Christ. Not just religion, but a transforming relationship with God that made a difference in every area of his life.

From the beginning, John's faith always had a practical edge to it, tied to real-world issues. For example, he started reaching out to men in prison. He quickly discovered that more than half the inmates were black. Then he discovered that most of them were from the South, including Mississippi. They had come west to escape

racism, just as John had, and just as I later would. But lacking education and therefore unable to cope in a new system, they inevitably
turned to crime. Eventually, they landed in prison.

John realized that if he genuinely wanted to intervene with God's
love in men's lives, he needed to do it before they left the South. In
fact, he needed to do it before they were grown up and desperate
to leave. So in an act of significant courage and faith, he returned
to Mississippi and founded a Christian community development
ministry in Mendenhall, called Voice of Calvary.

That's how I met him. John began working with the black young
people in Mendenhall, and occasionally he spoke at a chapel service
at Harper High School, where I attended.

Then one day my barber invited me to a tent meeting where
John was one of the speakers. I'll never forget that meeting, because John used flannelgraph to make his presentation. It was all
he had by way of audiovisuals! But it didn't matter, because John
himself was such an engaging speaker. Plus, something was going
on in my heart.

John was followed by another minister, Reverend Wallace. He
talked about all the things that God has done for us through Christ.
How every person in the world is born a sinner. And how, because
of our sin, we all deserve to be punished. Yet through Christ's death
on the cross, God offers us eternal life as a gift. God loves us and
wants to free us from our sin. He said a person could receive eternal
life just like receiving a gift. That you didn't have to *do* anything to
earn it or merit it. You could just accept it as God's gift to you.

As I say, something was stirring in my heart while I was listening to this message. It was the same thing John Perkins had heard
in California, the same powerful truth that had totally changed his
life. And so when Reverend Wallace invited those who wanted to

receive eternal life to come forward, I immediately went to the front of the tent.

All my life I'd worked hard to be good enough for God. I wasn't always certain that I was, but I'd sure tried. Now someone was telling me that regardless of how hard I worked at it, I was still a sinner. But through Christ, God was offering me salvation without having to work for it. Salvation was His gift to me. All I had to do was accept it. So I did. I prayed then and there. I told God I realized I was a sinner, and that my good works weren't good enough, but that if, because of Jesus' death on the cross, He was offering me forgiveness for my sins as a gift and eternal life as a gift, I would gladly and gratefully accept that offer. And so I became a Christian. I was convinced it was true. To this day I still am.

In the days and months that followed, I spent a lot of time with John Perkins and his coworkers at Voice of Calvary. I began attending classes that they offered on understanding the Bible and on how the gospel makes a difference in how one lives. It was not just moral instruction or personal betterment, although that was part of it. John had a way of bringing the Bible into many of the toughest issues we faced as black kids who were about to become adults, such as poverty, racism, politics, voting rights, and justice.

A Dream Come True

In the summer before my senior year of high school, John pulled me aside and said, "Dolphus, I'm driving out to California for a couple of weeks to visit some friends. Why don't you come with me?"

You have to try to imagine the impact of that suggestion on me! Except for my father's funeral in Louisiana, I had never been outside of Mississippi. What's more, I had never been outside of the Deep South. I had dreamed about leaving. I had talked about it.

But I'd never had the slightest opportunity to step outside of that oppressive world where I had grown up, let alone break free and "never come back." Now John Perkins was inviting me to go all the way to California.

Perhaps that trip more than anything else enabled me to believe that there really was a world outside of Mississippi, a whole different world that could offer me a whole different life than the one I'd grown up in. When I arrived in California and saw the orange groves, the freeways, the mountains, and the Pacific Ocean, I thought, "What am I doing here?" It was a question I would find myself asking again and again in my life. Something so wonderful was happening for me. Yet it was all so unbelievable.

Of course, it's one thing to visit the outside world; it's another thing to get there. In the fall, I started my senior year at Harper High, and after graduating, I eventually made it into Piney Woods Junior College. I knew I needed a college education, but I wasn't exactly sure what I was supposed to do with my life once I got one. I had a vague sense of wanting to go into the ministry. But not as a preacher! I'd had enough of the traditional black preachers like the ones I'd known growing up. I wanted to be able to handle the truth of the Bible with clarity and integrity. I also wanted to deal with the needs of the whole person in practical ways. In short, I wanted to do something along the lines of my role model, John Perkins. But what would that really look like? I didn't have the slightest idea.

However, if my future seemed totally unclear to me, it was perfectly known to God. I discovered that He was guiding my life in ways I never imagined. During my second year at Piney Woods, John arranged for a group of young men from California to speak at the school's chapel. One of them was David Nicholas, director of admissions at Los Angeles Baptist College (LABC).[1] I went up and introduced myself to him after the presentation. We talked for a while, and then he asked me, "Do you plan to finish college after Piney Woods?"

I didn't know what to say. I certainly wanted to get a four-year degree. I also was hoping to attend a Christian college. But there was one big problem that I couldn't get past: I wasn't aware of any Christian college that would accept blacks. Finally, I laid my cards on the table and told Dave about my misgivings.

He stunned me by replying, "How would you like to attend Los Angeles Baptist College?"

Now I was really at a loss for words! That was one of those times when the saying holds true, "Be careful what you wish for; you may just get it." Or better yet, "Be careful what you pray for; God may just give it to you." All my life I'd been wishing to leave Mississippi. I'd been hoping to get a college education at a Christian school. I'd been dreaming about paying for it through a basketball scholarship. I'd prayed about all of those things for hours. Now, through the conversation with Dave, God was beginning to answer my prayers.

You would think that I would have been overjoyed with getting accepted to LABC, and ecstatic upon receiving a basketball scholarship. But the truth is, I was scared to death! All the self-doubt, fear, and inferiority that I'd grown up with came back to haunt me. I seriously questioned whether I was equal to the challenge of LABC. What if I couldn't handle it academically? What if I didn't make the basketball team?

---

1. The school originally began as Los Angeles Baptist Theological Seminary and later expanded to include an undergraduate division called Los Angeles Baptist College, which since 1985 has been known as The Master's College.

In retrospect, I now realize that when God is leading my life, He doesn't seem to mind taking me into many situations that feel totally overwhelming and intimidating. I know He does it to build my faith. The situation turns out to be way too big for me, but it's never too big for God. He takes me way beyond what I thought I could handle—and sometimes even beyond what I know I can handle—so that I will trust *Him* to handle it. After all, wherever He leads me, He walks with me all the way.

A Dream Cut Short

That was certainly the case at LABC. It was great to be out of Mississippi and away from the rampant racism. But I discovered that racism also comes in more subtle forms—as always, from people who are scared or ignorant, or both.

One of the lowest points for me at LABC, and also a personal turning point, was the assassination of Dr. Martin Luther King Jr. on April 4, 1968. When someone told me about it, I ran to my room and flipped on the radio. I was shocked at what I was hearing, and all I could do was start praying.

But if I was shocked by the tragic news coming out of Memphis, I was horrified by the voices I overheard down the hall. Students were talking and even laughing about how glad they were that Martin Luther King had been shot! *"What?"* I wondered incredulously. "Am I in a foreign country? I thought this was America! I thought this was a Christian school! And here are these kids talking about how glad they are that Martin Luther King has been shot."

When the report finally came that Dr. King had died, a cheer went up from the kids down the hall. I couldn't tell who it was. I didn't want to. I just felt sick to my stomach. I kept wondering, "Isn't this supposed to be a Christian school? How can we even think about being happy over someone's death? How can we possibly be cheering or jumping for joy?"

In the moments that followed, I went through a lot of emotions as I sat in my room. There I was at a conservative, all-white, Christian liberal arts college of more than three hundred students. The only other black on campus was my friend Jimmie Walker. And we were the only two minorities in a town of fourteen thousand white folks. For a while, I thought that maybe hating white people for the rest of my life would be the right thing to do. I even toyed with the idea of leaving LABC and going to San Francisco to join up with H. Rap Brown and Stokely Carmichael and their "Black Power" movement. But in the end, God showed me that hate was not a viable option.

Instead, the Lord stirred Jimmie and me to pray earnestly about what we ought to do. In response, He showed us that racism is a much bigger and more basic problem than just a bunch of college kids joking around in a hallway. Those students were acting out of the ignorance and bigotry that had been passed on to them by families that had never dealt with the sin of prejudice. Prejudice, we began to see, can only be overcome by God's power. It's ultimately a spiritual issue.

Jimmie and I concluded that one important way God could begin to use us in addressing that issue was to open doors of understanding with our peers. We could become teachers as well as students on a campus dominated by white people. And so we intentionally became more active in speaking up and speaking out on behalf of black people's needs and issues. We hoped to stimulate conversation and to begin enlisting whites to work with us to overcome bigotry and racial animosity.

That kind of activism became my mission during the rest of that semester following Dr. King's death. I felt it was my calling—my assignment from God, if you will—to help the students and professors around me understand what black Americans were saying. I realized that many of them would someday take on leadership in their churches and communities and would influence countless others. Would theirs be an influence toward open-mindedness? Or would they enable their churches and communities to keep on saying that poverty and injustice are someone else's fault, and therefore someone else's responsibility?

Who knows how much I accomplished by those efforts. But as I accompanied my actions with prayer, I did begin to see breakthroughs with some of the students by the end of the school year. That lifted my hopes. Maybe Dr. King's dream of whites and blacks living in peace could become a reality after all. And maybe I could be an agent of change and reconciliation, just like Dr. King and John Perkins and other courageous leaders I admired.

An agent of change and reconciliation. Now that was a lofty aspiration! It sounded very noble. Very mature. Very courageous. There was just one small problem with that high-sounding vision: I wasn't anywhere near ready to take on that role just yet. I loved the idea of blacks and whites not only learning to "get along" with one another but even to understand and respect one another. That would truly be, as Dr. King envisioned, a dream come true. Yet the cold, hard reality was that, as much as I believed in that dream, I myself was not ready for change and reconciliation. Sure, I was advocating for it among my classmates and professors. But where was my own life headed? I had no idea, except for one thing: I was going to get as far away from Mississippi as I could.

And so, somewhat like Jonah in the Old Testament, the day came when I boarded a jet bound for Asia—all the way around the world from Mississippi! I was free at last.

Or so I thought.

CHAPTER 3

Miracles in Mendenhall

Just as basketball gave me a way out of Mississippi in the first place, basketball looked to be the way I could stay out for good.

After graduating from LABC, I went on to Los Angeles Baptist Theological Seminary. While there, I was approached by the mission organization Overseas Crusades. They were putting together a basketball team to tour Asia as a means of evangelistic outreach. They wanted me to join that team during the summer after my second year of seminary. I was deeply honored by the invitation—but stumped as to how I could possibly raise the $1,500 needed for my airfare.

Yet once again, as I mentioned in the previous chapter, when God is leading my life, the challenges He brings my way may be too big for me, but they're never too big for Him. In this case, He used the generosity of Christians in churches all over California to get behind me financially. I was stunned by their willingness to support a black man in ministry.

So I was on my way. I didn't really know what to expect as our plane headed out over the Pacific. But no matter how high anyone could have raised my expectations, what actually happened totally exceeded anything I could have imagined.

The purpose of the trip was evangelistic. Now having said that, you need to know that for me, proclaiming the gospel and working for racial reconciliation have never been competing interests but rather two sides of the same coin. That's been the case from the time I became a Christian.

Unfortunately, in the 1960s and '70s those two emphases often became separated. Some in the church claimed that winning souls, or "preaching the gospel," is and always should be the church's number-one priority. In effect, they would say, "What good does it do to alleviate poverty or pass laws against injustice if people end up in eternity without Christ?"

Meanwhile, other Christians would argue that all of our talk about God's love is meaningless unless we match our rhetoric with practical action that makes a real difference in people's day-to-day lives (i.e., working for racial reconciliation). After all, Christ Himself set an example of working with the poor. "The 'gospel' is nothing but a pie-in-the-sky fantasy until you put feet on it," those Christians would say. "Once poor people have food, clothing, shelter, and relief from injustice, then maybe they will be in a better position to hear more about our Jesus."

For my part, I don't believe I can legitimately pursue either emphasis without also pursuing the other. If I truly believe that Jesus sacrificed His very life in order to save people from their sins, then I cannot tell people about Jesus' love without also seeking to demonstrate that love in ways that address real needs—not just spiritual needs but material needs as well. I can't say to someone, "Jesus loves you" or "Jesus died for you" and then turn my back on the fact that they have no food in the house or no heat or no shoes to wear in the winter. Those were exactly the kinds of needs I and my brothers and sisters faced when we were growing up. We heard in church that God cared for our souls. But did He care for our bodies as well?

The book of James speaks precisely to that situation when it asks, "If a brother or sister is without clothing and in need of daily food, and one of you says to them, 'Go in peace, be warmed and be filled,' and yet you do not give them what is necessary for their body, what use is that?" (2:15–16 NASB).

But now, at the same time, I am cautious about swinging the pendulum in the opposite direction and making the gospel into nothing but a social services program. As I began to learn in the aftermath of Dr. King's assassination, racial reconciliation is ultimately a spiritual issue. Yes, racism manifests itself in ways that are very ugly and obvious. But if we only work on the social aspects of racism and never introduce the gospel, then we'll never see complete transformation. The gospel confronts racism's spiritual roots in sin and a broken relationship with God and with one another. If we neglect to proclaim the gospel, we'll never introduce people to the only One who can meet their deepest and ultimate need—their need for a Savior.

An Overwhelming Response

I can't pretend that I had all of this worked out in my mind and heart as I left on my mission trip to Asia. Indeed, it's been a lifelong journey for me to gain a better understanding of how the gospel speaks to both body and soul. All I knew when I landed in Taiwan was that many of the people I was going to meet had never even heard of Jesus. It was going to be my privilege to tell them about Him for the very first time.

What I hadn't bargained on was that I was also going to be the first black person many of them had ever seen. I was overwhelmed by their response. Our approach was to play three basketball games a day in a given location. After each game, members of the team would share their testimonies, and then we would invite those who wanted to learn more about Christ to stay and talk with us. Many of those who did so trusted Christ as their Savior. Then we would move to another location—sometimes many miles away—for the next day's games.

As I say, I was overwhelmed by the response of the Asians, not only to the gospel, but to *me!* Perhaps it was because I was the only black on the team. Perhaps it was because I was one of the shortest players on the team. Or perhaps it was because . . . well, could it be that God was revealing to me something of my own giftedness? Could it be that He was bringing to light a very natural way I seemed to have for getting people to respond to me, and through that response making an impact on their lives?

I'd never experienced such responsiveness from people before. At least, I'd never noticed it if I had. Certainly, in California people had listened politely to my early presentations of the gospel. Some of them had even put their faith in Christ as Savior. But here the response was amazing! Norm Cook, our coach, told us that God was doing a mighty work in Asia and that our mission trip would be a way to participate in what He was accomplishing. So I knew that what was happening was in no way the result of anything I was bringing to the party. And yet it did seem that God was using me in an unusual way to connect with people in Asia. If that were the case, could He be calling me to serve Him vocationally as a missionary in that part of the world?

Norm certainly thought so. Almost from the beginning of

our tour, he was convinced that I was born to preach the gospel to Asians. And each day seemed to confirm his suspicions. The crowds got bigger. The applause got stronger. More and more people responded to our gospel invitations. Meanwhile, our team had become a tight, loyal unit. And my own confidence as a speaker was soaring. I could actually begin to see myself doing that kind of work as a career.

Best of all was that I was on the other side of the world from Mississippi. Away from the poverty. Away from the racism. Away from the violence that even now was stalking John Perkins and my other friends back home. I felt badly for them, and I certainly kept them front and center in my prayers.

At the same time, I was discovering that poverty and racism are not limited to the southern United States. In Asia, I encountered people living in conditions far worse than what I had grown up in. That shocked me, because I had always thought I had lived in the worst of all possible circumstances. My circumstances as a boy were awful, to be sure. But the sins of racism and injustice extend worldwide, and through my trip to Asia my eyes were opened to just how desperately this entire planet needs a Savior.

Fear Not!

Obviously, God was using that trip to speak to my heart. But He was also using His Word, which is always the most important way He communicates His will to us. While I was in Asia, my girl-friend, Rosie, sent me a passage of Scripture to focus on: "Keep reading Psalm 91," she told me. And so, night after night, I read and meditated on Psalm 91 as I lay on my bunk after the day's ministry. It begins:

He who dwells in the secret place of the Most High
Shall abide under the shadow of the Almighty.
   I will say of the LORD, "He is my refuge and my fortress;
My God, in Him I will trust."
   Surely He shall deliver you from the snare of the fowler
And from the perilous pestilence.
   He shall cover you with His feathers,
And under His wings you shall take refuge;
His truth shall be your shield and buckler. (vv. 1–4 NKJV)

I pondered those words and kept trying to apply them to our evangelistic tour in Asia. Certainly we needed God's protection, and we needed to hold onto our trust in Him. Yet we never actually felt any danger during our trip. There was nothing going on to make us afraid. Sure, we sometimes felt nervous getting up in front of hundreds of people and sharing our testimonies, especially in the early going. But were we ever really threatened by "the snare of the fowler"? (In biblical times, fowlers were bird-catchers who used nets to ensnare their quarry.) Were we ever really endangered by "the perilous pestilence" (meaning a serious disease, like leprosy or the plague)?

The more I reflected on the passage, the less I felt it was speaking to our trip to Asia. Rather, it seemed to be speaking to me about Mississippi. If ever there was a place where a person needed God to be his or her refuge, shield, and buckler (or armor), it was in Mississippi.

Then one day God impressed upon me that the reason I needed Him as my refuge was because I was allowing fear to drive my life. Fear of poverty. Fear of injustice. Fear of violence. Fear of Mississippi.

I had grown up in a broken system, and I had developed an anger against that system, a rage that ultimately drove me to get out of the South and swear that I'd never go back. But underneath that anger and that rage was fear. Fear that nothing could ever change. Fear that the situation there was hopeless. Fear that no one really cared.

Through Psalm 91, God was reassuring me: "I care! I care about *you*, Dolphus. I know you're scared and that you're running away. But Dolphus, you don't need to run away. You're black, and I love you. You were born in the South, and I love you. You don't need to run away from your blackness or the fact that you're from the South. In Me, you are safe. In Me, you have security."

That was it! Like Jonah, I was running away from everything I most feared. Yes, I was doing good work in Asia, and God was certainly blessing my team's efforts. But I was still running *away* from Mendenhall and all that Mendenhall represented. I was not running *toward* something else. It was a strategy based on fear, not on the confidence of a calling. I realized that if I was running away, then no matter how far I ran, I could never run away from the Mendenhall inside of me, the one in my head and in my heart. Until I could trust God to be my refuge there, I would always be en-slaved to fear and a sense of hopelessness, because only God could overcome that despair. Only God could give me a lasting hope—not just for a better house or a better job or a better life, all of which are legitimate desires. But they are not what ultimately matters. Only God could give me a hope for becoming the person He had created me to be.

God was doing business with me there in Asia. He had taken me all the way to the other side of the world—to show me what? That He loved me. That He was committed to protecting me. That He was fully aware of how desperate things were back in Mississippi.

And also that He had plans for my life. To my utter surprise, I felt Him urging me, "Dolphus, I have something for you to do in Mississippi."

It was not exactly what I wanted to hear! I felt weighed down with the prospect of returning to my roots. It wasn't just the active racism of the system that troubled me. That I could fight against. But what was I going to do about all of the black people I knew who just accepted the situation with the attitude, "There's nothing you can do, nothing is ever going to change, it's hopeless"?

Once again, God's promises in Psalm 91 spoke to my fears:

> Because he has set his love upon Me, therefore I will deliver him;
>> I will set him on high, because he has known My name.
>> He shall call upon Me, and I will answer him;
>> I will be with him in trouble;
>> I will deliver him and honor him.
>>> With long life I will satisfy him,
>>> And show him My salvation. (vv. 14–16 NKJV)

If God was committed to delivering me from any troubles I might face back at home, then how could I not return? Indeed, for me to pursue an evangelistic career in Asia seemed selfish, no matter how fruitful my work there had been so far. It would actually be self-serving, because I knew that if I was ministering in Asia as a way to stay free of Mississippi, I would be doing it for what I was getting out of it, not for the sake of the Asians. By contrast, returning home would require genuine sacrifice on my part. That meant it would genuinely be for the sake of the people there, not just for my own happiness.

There was no single moment when the decision was made to de-vote my life to Mississippi. All I know is that whereas I was run-ning away from Mississippi on the flight to Asia, I was committed to returning to Mississippi on the flight back to the United States.

The first thing I did when I got home was to marry Rosie (more on that later). Then we headed back to Los Angeles for me to fin-ish seminary. And then, upon graduation in the spring of 1971, I with my new wife did what I swore I'd never do: I returned to Mendenhall.

Where to Begin?

It was far from a triumphant homecoming. Things were in con-siderable disarray. John Perkins and his family had more or less been forced to move to Jackson. Constant pressure from the au-thorities, an ineffective court system that crept along at a snail's pace, bomb threats and other violence against his person, and countless other challenges had taken a severe toll on John's health. Despite John's absence, the folks in Mendenhall had managed to maintain a tutoring program and radio ministry. But there was no question that the future of the ministry that John had pioneered was in doubt.

Faced with those daunting realities, I started to wonder, "Is this really where God wants me?" I felt like Nehemiah when he learned that the walls of his hometown, Jerusalem, were broken down and the people who remained were in great distress. But remarkably, instead of the fear, anger, and hopelessness I had felt upon leaving my hometown just a few years earlier, I now had a quiet confidence and peace that God was with me as I returned. I felt a deep convic-tion that, yes, I was right where God wanted me—right back in Mendenhall, Mississippi!

So where should I begin? Given that John's work in Mendenhall had nearly cost him his life, we decided it would be best for him to focus on traveling and raising money, while I would take his place on-site to implement strategy. As I prayed about what to do first, it didn't take long for the Lord to show me the obvious answer: start with the youth. We needed to start with our young people because children and teenagers are malleable. They may be struggling with poverty, but they are not yet trapped by the hopeless thinking that cycles of poverty create in poor people's minds as they get older. Young people still dream of change. They haven't quite given up, in contrast to the adults who have had their hopes dashed so many times that they can no longer seize genuine opportunities when they come along or even recognize them as hopeful possibilities.

Starting with the youth meant starting with their education. Education was a huge need because blacks had become significantly disadvantaged, ironically, as a result of the desegregation of Mississippi's schools in the early 1970s. When the schools became integrated, almost all of the black students were way behind their white counterparts right from the beginning. That's because the quality of instruction and materials in the all-black schools they had come from had generally been poor.

There was also the problem of child labor, which had a way of pitting basic education against basic survival. Most black parents wanted their children to graduate from high school. But it was hard to make education a priority when a family was struggling to make ends meet. The large cotton and corn farms in Simpson County required a large labor pool. Black families supplied that labor, including their children, beginning at about age ten. In April, the planting of the crops began. In late August, the harvest started coming in, which meant that many kids didn't show up for school until around Thanksgiving. Needless to say, they remained hopelessly behind the other students.

On top of that legacy, the constant drip-drip-drip of racism in the wider culture ate like acid at the self-esteem of black children, creating an "I'm-no-good" mind-set. And racism in the workplace defeated efforts at any kind of learning and self-improvement by denying black students the rewards of self-discipline and honest achievement.

As a result of these challenges, black students were giving up on education. Most were dropping out of school with a "what's-the-use" attitude.

We started small, offering tutoring classes in English, math, black history, Bible, and art. At first it seemed like an exercise in futility. We were reaching out to the poorest children in Simpson County, many of them living in falling-down shacks along rutted dirt roads. All we had to transport them to our program were beat-up vans running on bald tires, with recycled engines that were constantly breaking down. We had a typing class, but not enough working typewriters. We had a reading class, but not enough books. We tutored them in writing, but oftentimes we had to share pencils. And if too many students showed up, we didn't have enough chairs for everyone.

So what kept us going? On some days, nothing but a sheer stubborn trust that because God wanted us to do what we were doing, He would not let us down. He would vindicate our efforts with real results. On other days, we felt more desperate. We only stayed the course because to quit would have been to give in to despair and the debilitating "nothing-is-ever-going-to-change" mentality.

In the end, of course, what kept us going was God. He encouraged us with small but real victories. Kids who had been missing too many days of school started to show regular attendance. Kids who had been making Ds and Fs began making Bs and even As. One teenage girl who had been shy and withdrawn began to emerge as a leader and even started tutoring some of the younger children.

Eventually, she graduated from high school, which was a huge victory and a tremendous encouragement for the other kids in the community. "See? If she can do it, so can you!" And then the day came when she graduated from college. That made her a real role model! She had proven that the dream could come true.

A Total Transformation

Yes, the dream could come true for an individual. But what about for an entire community? One of the things we Christians who take the gospel seriously need to wrestle with is what we mean when we say that the gospel can "transform" lives. How far-reaching is that transformation? Is it just for individuals? Or can an entire system be changed?

Look at it this way. When I returned to Simpson County in 1971, a majority of black students were dropping out of school before graduating. Many were quitting after the compulsory level of fifth grade (and the laws were not enforced for some who left even earlier than that). The dropouts were almost inevitably doomed to lives of poverty.

For many of the young men, it also meant crime, which of course would lead to prison. What did the gospel have to say to that? Through our ministry at Mendenhall, we were privileged to intervene in a number of kids' lives. Many of them turned the corner and ended up getting a good education, with the result that today they are living productive lives. Praise God for that!

But could we really say that our gospel was *transforming* education in our community, when a majority of the black students were still dropping out? To my way of thinking, *transformation* means more than helping individuals here and there. It means changing the way a system works so no one has to break out of that system in order to get what is rightfully theirs to begin with. I wondered, "What would it look like to *transform* the educational system for black children in Mendenhall and Simpson County?"

I prayed about this issue for years: "Lord, what can we do about the education of black children here? You know that most of them are behind from the start of their schooling. How will they ever catch up? And those who stay in school are learning a lot of values that seem opposed to Your ways. What can we do about this?"

What made those prayers all the more urgent was the presence of an abandoned, two-story, cinder-block building in the Black Quarters of Mendenhall (the low-lying section of town across the railroad tracks next to the creek where most of the black families lived). At one time, that building had been Harper High School, the first high school for blacks in Simpson County. Black families had made five- and ten-dollar contributions to buy the property on which it sat and the individual blocks from which it was built. Now the structure sat vacant, its windows broken out, and its yard full of weeds. It was a terrible eyesore. Even worse, it was a terrible "mindsore," an insulting reminder that blacks were always going to be the losers in a broken and unjust educational system.

What our kids needed was a *transformation* in their educational outlook! So in 1976, the leaders of our ministry began talking and praying about a nursery school for children of low-income parents. Nothing like that was available elsewhere in the area. In an amazing answer to our prayers, two students—a black male and a white female, both of whom had just received their degrees in education—contacted us from Wheaton College in Wheaton, Illinois. John Perkins had spoken at Wheaton and shared the vision for a school in Mendenhall. Independent of one another, those two students responded to his message and wrote to ask if we'd be interested in their help to start the school. Obviously, we said yes. So they moved to Mendenhall and spent six months preparing to open a nursery school for two- and three-year-olds. Once it was up and running, they introduced a kindergarten class, enrolling thirteen children for half-day sessions.

We called the program Genesis One Christian School Kindergarten. The name emphasized our desire to give kids a proper education "from the beginning." Of course, the real test of whether we were accomplishing that vision came when our first "graduates" began moving into first grade at the public school. To our delight, the Genesis One kids earned high ratings on the school's assessment test for incoming first graders.

That success quickly raised parents' expectations, and soon we were being asked, "Why don't you have a first grade too? If you do, we'll support it." Their promise of support was no small thing. You have to realize that the families our school was serving were only making between $7,000 and $12,000 a year. The median income in our area was barely $6,000. To make school affordable, we charged $6 a week per child. Fundraising made up the difference. But now the parents were starting to see real results from their investment. So they were eager to see the program expand.

In response to that demand, the Lord raised up Judi Adams, the wife of Dr. Dennis Adams, a young black physician who had intentionally chosen to set up his medical practice in Mendenhall in order to provide affordable health care to our community. Judi had a background in education, and she did extensive research to develop the idea of a Christian grade school for grades 1 through 3—and someday grades 4 and up, Lord willing.

The parents were very excited to hear about this vision. But how would they ever be able to afford it? We estimated the cost at $1,400 per child per year—an impossible sum! After a lot of number crunching and prayer, we came up with a tuition figure of $525 a year, which meant we'd have to raise about $900 per student per year over and above that amount to cover all the costs. However, because enough parents agreed to that fee, we formally expanded Genesis One in the fall of 1982 to grades 1 through 3. Twenty-five children attended the kindergarten program, and ten children enrolled in the elementary classes. The next fall we added fourth grade, and enrollment doubled to seventy-five students.

That created a space problem. Our temporary solution was to spread out the classes among buildings throughout the community. But we knew that arrangement would not last for long.

It seemed to me that now was the time to reclaim that abandoned cinder-block building where Harper High once held classes. It was the perfect size for what we needed. But how in the world could that happen, since it would take at least $25,000 to restore the building for our purposes?

A New Day for Mendenhall

I still tingle every time I think about what happened next. I shared our vision for the building with a group of volunteers who were visiting from Aurora Christian School in Aurora, Illinois. They sized up what we needed, and when their spring break came around, they brought 160 students and adults to Mendenhall to give the building a complete makeover. It was like a reality TV show! Imagine hundreds of workers scurrying around and inside and on top of the building, tearing out old walls, hammering together studs for new frames, putting in new windows, hanging doors, painting walls, sealing cracks, and carting away debris. After a week of feverish labor, the work was complete. The contrast between "before" and "after" could not have been more extreme.

Then a few days later, a group from Second Presbyterian Church in Memphis came in and graded and fenced the playground. When they returned home, a woman in their church heard about the project and donated $8,000 of playground equipment. About that same time, a couple from Jackson gave $10,000 to furnish the kitchen.

On August 10, 1984, we dedicated the Genesis One Christian School facility. The mayor of Mendenhall came. The board of our ministry was there. The group from Aurora came back to participate. Scores of folks from all over Simpson County were on hand. An impossible dream had come true! The building was there. The students were there. The funding was there. God had performed a miracle in Mendenhall. He had created hope where there had been no hope.

Now that's what I call *transformation!* Transformation means a complete reversal. It means a 180-degree turnaround in the way things are happening. It means that a system that used to function one way starts to function in an entirely different way. In short, transformation means a new day. It's what the prophet Isaiah said would happen when the Messiah was to come:

> The people who walk in darkness
>   Will see a great light;
>   Those who live in a dark land,
>   The light will shine on them. (Isa. 9:2 NASB)

The Genesis One Christian School brought a very bright light into a very dark corner of Mississippi. Did it solve all of our problems? Of course not. *But it substantially changed the way black kids in Simpson County get started in education.* That has made a huge difference. It means more black kids are entering public school at the same educational level as their white peers. It means fewer black kids are dropping out, and more are graduating from high school. That, in turn, means that more black students are going on to vocational schools, junior colleges, and four-year colleges. Some of them are ending up in graduate schools. A number have ended up in the professions, in business, in government, and in education. It means educated young people live in Simpson County as productive citizens who are able to give back to their community. In short, it means that a transformation has taken place.

The wonderful thing for me is that Genesis One Christian School is but one of many miracles God has done in Mendenhall. I could also tell you about how He brought us the health clinic mentioned earlier. About the community law office He raised up. About the way He provided the R. A. Buckley Recreational Center, where we started programs targeted at youth. He helped us start a thrift store where poor folks can buy quality merchandise at an affordable price. He blessed us with a cooperative farm and an adult education program. He helped us work in conjunction with Mendenhall Bible Church to start a Pastors Development Program and a Christian Youth Leadership Development initiative. Beyond all of this, He allowed us to provide technical assistance and support to countless ministries similar to ours all around the country.

What's Next?

I could go on and on about all of the miracles God has done to bring the transforming presence of the gospel to Simpson County. Many of those stories you can find in my first book, *I Ain't Comin' Back.* If you read that book, you'll understand more of the background behind the rest of the story to come. It will also help you understand how it came about that I was invited to stand on the tarmac at NAS Meridian to greet the president of the United States and receive, on behalf of Mendenhall Ministries, a Point of Light Award.

Six groups were receiving the award that day. Ours was the only black organization represented. It was also the only Christian ministry. And it was the only program aimed at the rural poor. It was just an awesome feeling to stand there. Awesome and, frankly, sobering. Why us? Rosie and I had been just two poor people from rural Mississippi. Now here we were, representing the kind of hope that poor people can have through faithfulness to a vision, faithfulness to God, and faithfulness to do what we believed God had called us to do.

As I say, it was an awesome moment. I felt the way a quarterback must feel after winning the Super Bowl. That awesome sense of exhilaration when you realize your team has done what it set out to do, and everyone is cheering and celebrating that accomplishment. Then someone jabs a microphone in your face and shouts, "So Dolphus, now that you've won the Super Bowl, what are you going to do next?"

Of course the proper thing to say is, "I'm taking my family to Disney World!"

And that's exactly what happened. A few months later, President

Bush invited all of the Points of Light Award–winners and their families to Disney World. It was a delightful time, especially for my daughter, Danita, and my sons, Reggie and Ryan. The organizers even took a picture of all the award winners with President and Mrs. Bush. And through that honor, I ended up with my picture in the paper!

However, the Super Bowl analogy breaks down at this point, because I never saw our Point of Light Award as the Vince Lombardi Trophy, given to the winning team at end of the Super Bowl. I never felt as if we'd finished our game. To my mind, the Point of Light Award was more like stopping for halftime. Our team may have played a great first half, and perhaps we could even say that we were ahead in the score. But there was still a lot more game to be played. It felt great to have someone as important as the president tell us we were playing well. But the contest was far from over.

So as soon as I got back from Disney World, I started praying a new prayer: "Okay, Lord, what do you want me to do next?"

CHAPTER 4

"I Can't Never Leave!"

I think I would have been asking the question, *What's next?* whether or not we received the Point of Light Award. That honor just happened to come along at a point in my career when I was already starting to think about what my best use might be.

I was so pleased with what was going on in Mendenhall. As I indicated in the previous chapter, our programs were making a real difference for black folks in our community. We had an outstanding team of leaders heading up our ministry. Volunteers from all over the United States were regularly coming in to help us with various projects, and we viewed their visits as opportunities to minister to them, not just to be ministered to. Perhaps most important of all, I was seeing significant progress being made in the relationship between whites and blacks in Simpson County. Not that there still weren't problems. But the open racism I had experienced growing up was definitely on the wane. And the way racial issues were being addressed was becoming much more civil and constructive.

In the years following the Point of Light recognition, I began to travel more and to serve on national boards. I also consulted with groups in various urban communities around the country that wanted to adapt The Mendenhall Ministry as a model for their ministries. Those activities put me more in touch with my gifts of encouraging and motivating others. I learned that I'm more of a visionary/dreamer than someone who runs the day-to-day operations of an organization.

In light of that, the TMM board encouraged me to bring in Cecil Essix to become TMM's first vice president during the early 1990s. Then in 1992, God brought us Shelby Smith from Arkansas to serve as the executive vice president. For the next three years, as I traveled around the country and Shelby oversaw the organization, TMM enjoyed some of its greatest success.

Telling "The Mendenhall Story"

One of the most valuable tools I had in telling that story was my book *I Ain't Comin' Back*. Back in 1982, Dr. Kevin Lake, one of TMM's board members, started encouraging me to write a book about my story and tell about what God was doing in Mendenhall. That sounded like a great idea, but there was just one problem: I've never been much of a writer.

Fortunately, God had already provided the perfect answer to that problem in Chris Erb. Chris was the very first volunteer our ministry ever had. Beginning in 1969, and for the next eight summers, she came at her own expense from Massachusetts to Mendenhall to organize youth activities, tutor children, and do whatever else she could to aid our efforts. After she talked to me during her volunteering time, she recognized that there was a book waiting to be written in Mendenhall. She began to tape-record conversations with my mother and others who had known me for years. From those interviews she cobbled together the beginnings of a manuscript.

That's when God brought Bea Shira into my life. Bea was a member of the Second Presbyterian Church in Memphis. She had a background in publishing and editing, and she took Chris's work and developed it into a more mature form.

Nevertheless, the project never quite resulted in a published book. Perhaps it was because we were just a small ministry in a tiny rural town. The publishers wanted books that would attract tens and hundreds of thousands of readers. Who would buy a book about a community of black folk in a little hamlet in Mississippi?

In the late 1980s, Gary Bauer, a video producer from Dallas, Texas, and a member of our board, suggested that we create a video about our ministry that could be used for fundraising purposes. Gary recruited his friend Bill Hendricks to serve as the producer for that video. After completing the project, Bill said to me the same thing Kevin Lake had said a few years earlier: "Dolphus, you need to get your story into a book." I told him we had a book. At least, we had a manuscript.

Bill was already a published author, with several books to his credit. After he read over the work that Chris and Bea had done, he insisted on taking over our book project and getting it into print. I was overjoyed by his enthusiasm and willingness to help. But I was a bit hesitant, because I knew we had no money to pay him. "I'm not expecting to get paid," he shot back when I told him that. "I'll do it for free." I was dumbfounded. "Dolphus," he explained, "I don't have the means to write you a big check. If I did, I would. But what I do have is an ability to write. So let me offer that as my contribution to what you are doing. We'll need to have both of our names on the cover as authors, since that has more integrity than if I just ghostwrite it for you. But whatever royalties come in from the sale of the book, I want them to go to Mendenhall." And with that, he went to work.

About a year later, Tyndale House agreed to publish our manuscript, and in the fall of 1990, the first copies of *I Ain't Comin' Back* arrived. Another dream come true!

We immediately put that dream to work. We sent out notices to our entire constituency that "the Mendenhall story," as we called it, was finally available in print. We urged everyone to buy at least two copies: one for their own use, and one to give to a friend, a church leader, or a church library. We wanted our story to inspire Christians everywhere to take seriously what the gospel has to say about the poor and about racial reconciliation. Wherever I went in my travels, I brought along a box of books. Amazingly, I usually had sold all of them before I left.

As a result of those efforts, the Mendenhall story reached places I never could have imagined. We began receiving letters from all over the country from people who wanted to reproduce in their communities what we were doing in ours.

From the beginning, I determined that all of the proceeds from book sales should go into a special fund to underwrite scholarships for Genesis One students. My mother had a fierce commitment to seeing that all of her children got as good an education as they possibly could—so much so that people used to say she was "education crazy." Well, I'm thankful she was, because it made me "education crazy" as well. Even though I say basketball opened the door for me to a better life, the truth is that basketball paid for my education, and it was my education that opened the door to a better life. I wanted education to open that same door for the kids in Mendenhall, which is why we started Genesis One in the first place.

A Change of Seasons

Without question, the book raised my profile among Christian ministries. God was the One who had caused me to see racism as a spiritual issue and taught me that proclaiming the gospel of Jesus Christ and working for racial reconciliation were two sides of the same coin. Now these ideas with the challenges they bring to our Christian faith were published for others to consider. Many other ministries were beginning to examine their positions on racial issues. And a number of them recognized that they would have a hard time working across racial lines unless they placed people from other races into positions of leadership. More and more, I was being asked to participate in conversations about these matters. The attention was both humbling and exciting! Eventually, I was honored to serve on the board of InterVarsity Christian Fellowship, later World Vision, and more recently, the Evangelical Council for Financial Accountability, among others.

I was also starting to get phone calls from recruiters, asking if I would allow my name to be considered for a leadership role at this or that ministry. It was very flattering to think that well-known ministries would think that much of me. But I wasn't really interested in leaving Mendenhall.

Or was I? Maybe the best way to put it is that while I was in no way thinking about leaving Mendenhall, I was wondering if the calls I was getting were God's way of telling me He wanted me to do something else. Maybe after twenty-six years in Mendenhall, I had completed the work He had sent me there to do. That seemed plausible. But if so, what was I supposed to do next? I had no clear answer for that, though it did cause a lot of soul-searching.

One clue that the season was changing, however, was a growing disagreement between me and the other leaders of our ministry over how TMM should be governed. Not that we were in conflict over it. But we had a philosophical difference of opinion.

TMM had grown out of Mendenhall Bible Church (MBC) as a means of reaching beyond the church's walls to serve the surrounding community. The organization had its own budget, and in time developed its own board. I was the president of the ministry and also served as an elder of the church. Artis Fletcher, the pastor of MBC, served as the chairman of the board for the ministry.

The point of disagreement was over the church's authority in relation to the ministry. We all agreed that the ministry should be accountable to the church in terms of spiritual authority and doctrine. But I, on the one hand, believed that from a legal and governance standpoint, TMM should be a separate 501(c)(3) entity. I didn't think TMM's eighteen-member board, which included people from across the United States, should be accountable to the board of a local church. I also felt that donors to the ministry, especially churches, would not feel right about contributing resources to a parachurch ministry that answered to another church. The leadership of MBC, on the other hand, believed that since TMM had started as an extension of the church, the church should retain complete control over the ministry, including oversight of the ministry's board.

After a lot of discussion and prayer on this matter, the elders decided to create a different model. The church membership, which was the membership of the ministry as well, voted to add ten members from the church to the board of directors of TMM, and they asked some of the national board members to step down. That created a board that was dominated by church members, giving Mendenhall Bible Church ultimate control of TMM.

This decision also opened the door for me to transition out of my role as president of TMM. I firmly believed that the elders were godly men who had prayerfully arrived at their decision for the new form of governance. I also felt that Tim Keyes, who had become TMM's vice president, had the potential to lead the ministry under the new structure. Looking back, I can see now that God was teaching me more about trusting Him and trusting others, especially through seasons of change.

A Change of Heart

All of these developments forced me to ask the question, *So what does God want me to do next?* I had no clear direction for what that might be. But the experience of thinking and praying about it caused me to revisit my feelings about Mississippi. For the first two decades of my life, I had dreamed and schemed to get out of Mississippi, with no intention of ever coming back. Then, when I was all the way on the other side of the world, God got ahold of my heart and showed me that Mississippi was exactly where I needed to be and that He had a great work in store for me there. So I had come back and given twenty-six years to TMM. But what about now? Did I still want to leave Mississippi?

As I searched my heart, I quickly realized that the old desire to go elsewhere was gone. Somehow—exactly *when*, I couldn't pinpoint— my heart had changed. I no longer felt bitter toward Mississippi, the way I had growing up. Somehow God had transformed my bitterness into compassion. I actually felt compassion, not only for black folks who were trying to recover from the wrongs of the past, but also for white folks who were also working to overcome historical racial barriers.

It wasn't a compassion of sentimentality or feeling sorry for people. Rather, it was a compassion that was calling me to action. I was *frustrated* about the racial divide. Poignant words from a sermon preached in 1953 expressed the essence of my frustration: "I am ashame[d] and appalled that Eleven O'clock on Sunday morning is the most segregated hour in Christian America."[1] I felt especially pained that more Christians didn't seem to realize that in Christ, there is no black or white. As the Scripture says, "There is neither Jew nor Greek, slave nor free, male nor female, for you are all one in Christ Jesus" (Gal. 3:28; cf. Col. 3:11). As believers we are new creations. That sets us free from the old distinctions, and with them, the old prejudices. That now seemed as clear as day to me. Why couldn't everyone else—and especially everyone in the church—"get it"?

Sometimes getting worked up over something is a sure sign that *you* are the one who should do something about it. I began to wonder if that wasn't the case for me. I was feeling very passionate about the need for racial reconciliation. Certainly I knew about that issue firsthand. Was God calling me to serve Him in some way in that area?

All the time I was wrestling with this question, I continued to receive inquiries from other ministries that were interested in me. I looked into a number of those opportunities, and I have to admit, some of them looked very appealing. But none of them were in Mississippi. And to my surprise—and ultimately to my delight—I found myself backing away from each one *precisely because none of them were in Mississippi!* In other words, I discovered that God had completely transformed my heart. Earlier in my life, I had fled Mississippi with the vow, "I ain't never comin' back!" But then God called me back, and I obeyed. Now, to my utter amazement, I was declaring, "I can't never leave!" I'd never felt such freedom!

---

1. Quoted from a sermon titled "Communism's Challenge to Christianity" (August 9, 1953) in Martin Luther King Jr., *The Papers of Martin Luther King, Jr.*, Vol. 6, *Advocate of the Social Gospel, September 1948–March 1963* (Berkeley: University of California Press, 2007), 149.

That insight changed my prayers considerably. I was no longer asking, "Lord, what do you want me to do next?" but rather, "Lord, what do you want me to do next *in Mississippi*?" That narrowed the field considerably. Especially when I was able to put the place (Mississippi) together with the cause (racial reconciliation). Where was God doing something involving racial reconciliation in the state of Mississippi?

A New Mission in Mississippi

I didn't have to look far. Just a couple of years earlier in 1995, I had agreed to sit on the board of a fledgling organization in Jackson called Mission Mississippi. It was still more of a movement than a full-fledged ministry. Its executive director had only been on board for about a year, and the formal entity had only been in existence for about two years.

The beginnings of Mission Mississippi dated to 1993. In response to a number of painfully obvious social problems in the Jackson area, a handful of ministers and concerned laypeople, both blacks and whites, began meeting for a prayer breakfast every Thursday morning. They specifically prayed for God to help them find ways to overcome the various prejudices and injustices that were continuing to poison our state. No one in that initial group could say exactly why they felt they needed to be intentional about coming together across racial lines to pray together. Nor did they have any idea what they thought God was going to do through their meetings. They just knew that somebody had to "do something." Coming together to ask for God's guidance seemed like one way of "doing something."

Little did they realize that God was already responding to their prayers through a Christian men's fellowship. Months before those prayer meetings even started, a businessman named Lee Paris, chairman and CEO of Mississippi Properties, had attended the 1990 SEC Basketball Tournament in Orlando, Florida. On that trip, he met Pat Morley. Pat was a very successful real estate developer. He was also the author of a best-selling book, *The Man in the Mirror*, which spoke to men about developing a deeper relationship with God. Lee and Pat became fast friends.

Impressed by Pat's story, Lee invited Pat to visit Jackson and speak to the Christian Businessmen's Committee, a fellowship group in which Lee was an active participant. Pat did so, and soon he became a regular visitor and speaker to that group.

In time, Pat expressed a desire to lead a citywide evangelistic crusade in Jackson. But the group decided to pass on that idea. They loved Pat's ministry to their smaller group, but they were unsure how well he would fare in a larger, citywide effort.

When Lee contacted Pat to inform him of the group's decision, he assumed that Pat would be deeply disappointed. To his surprise, however, Pat said, "Okay, then how would you feel about me and my best friend, Tom Skinner, coming to lead an event to deal with the need for Christian unity?" Tom was a black minister who had grown up on the streets of Harlem before God got ahold of him and transformed his life.

The men's group was much more open to that idea, but they realized they weren't equipped to host such an event on their own. So Lee Paris and Victor Smith, another highly respected businessman in the group, organized a luncheon in November 1992 for ministers and lay leaders across the city. About 130 people showed up to hear Pat Morley and Tom Skinner talk about their vision for a Christian unity event.

Whatever else the crowd was expecting to hear that day, they hadn't bargained on what actually happened. Pat and Tom did more than just cast a vision. They spoke openly and personally about their own lives and about the deep friendship they shared. In fact, they declared that their commitment to one another was so genuine and strong that, if necessary, they would willingly lay down their lives for one another. That was not just an idle boast. Tom Skinner had been a gang leader as a youth. He knew all about putting one's life on the line out of loyalty to a friend.

The friendship between Tom and Pat was reminiscent of the kind of covenant loyalty David and Jonathan shared in the Old Testament. Yet unlike David and Jonathan, who were from the same ethnic group, here was a black Baptist Democrat from Harlem and a white Presbyterian Republican from Florida expressing total devotion to one another. No one at the luncheon had ever seen such a bold demonstration of Christian unity and love.

When it came time to respond to what Pat and Tom were suggesting, the group affirmed that instead of a large evangelistic crusade in Jackson, the city desperately needed to hear how the gospel could lead people to have relationships like the one Pat and Tom had—relationships built on Christian love and trust, transcending race or church affiliation.

In order to start acting on the challenge Pat and Tom had given the group, another meeting was held a month later, and a steering committee was formed to start planning for an event. A tentative date was set for October 1993. However, the planners quickly realized that just holding a one-time event would do very little to achieve all that needed to be done to heal the racial divide in Jackson. An event could be a great kickoff, but the group would need to commit to a longer-term strategy if it hoped to make a real and lasting difference.

It was during one of those early meetings that a minister voiced a key insight: "If the whole church is going to come together to reach Jackson with the gospel, shouldn't the whole church be represented in planning this event?" His suggestion was so obvious that everyone felt a bit sheepish for not recognizing it earlier. Yet to that point, the planning group was largely comprised of white leaders, with only a few leaders from the black community. As a result of that minister's challenge, the group decided that if it wanted to accomplish anything worthwhile, it was going to have to make every effort to bring the *whole* church together and involve leaders from every part of the Christian community, regardless of racial or denominational lines. Only a radical commitment to unity in Christ would make any sort of meaningful statement to the city of Jackson.

And that was the beginning of Mission Mississippi. The steering committee for the citywide event became the steering committee for a broader, longer-term movement aimed at racial reconciliation based on the gospel. The initial rally with Pat Morley and Tom Skinner proved to be an exciting, historic event, resulting in countless changed lives and a renewed sense of hope among Christians for the future of Mississippi. The gathering also turned out to be one of the last major events Tom participated in before his death in 1994.

From an Event to a Movement to a Ministry

During those first days, when Mission Mississippi was being birthed, a man named Jim Hitt played an instrumental role in providing leadership and getting the group headed in the right direction. Jim did a superb job of brokering relationships between churches, ministries, businesses, and nonprofit organizations throughout the Jackson area.

Then, after about a year of activity and as it became apparent that

God indeed had His hand on these fledgling efforts and was form-ing the movement into a ministry, the steering committee invited one of its own, Jarvis Ward, to become Mission Mississippi's first executive director. Jarvis, whose background was in sales and mar-keting, had been the director of special ministries at the New Lake Outreach Center in Jackson's inner city.

Initially, Jarvis was hesitant about accepting a brand new role with a brand new and relatively unproven organization whose fu-ture was by no means clear. But as he prayed about it, God helped him realize he could have a greater impact on a larger number of people through Mission Mississippi. And so it was. For three years God powerfully used Jarvis to turn a well-intentioned cause into a solid, thriving ministry that was making a real difference and see-ing real results in our state's capital city.

I came on the board about a year after Jarvis assumed the execu-tive director position. I was completely sold on Mission Mississippi's vision and believed wholeheartedly that God was going to use the organization to transform race relations in our state. I was particu-larly delighted that my friend and mentor John Perkins was also be-ing invited to serve on the board. I felt honored to partner with him again, along with so many other great Christian leaders, in further-ing a cause I and others had been championing for three decades in Mendenhall.

All of these developments with Mission Mississippi were tak-ing place at about the same time that Mendenhall Bible Church and TMM were sorting out their governance relationship. When the vote came down on the side of having the TMM board subor-dinate to the board of the church, I knew that I was entering my final days as president of TMM. As I mentioned earlier, I was not actively looking for another assignment, but I did have ministries contacting me. And I suppose my openness to other possibilities must have been apparent to other leaders with whom I associated— including the board at Mission Mississippi.

Three years after Jarvis became our executive director, he was "stolen away" by a national ministry called the Mission America Coalition, a cross-denominational initiative aimed at mobilizing the church to pray, care, and share the gospel in deed and word. Of course I'm joking when I say Mission America stole him away. The truth is, a man of Jarvis's talents is always a hot commodity, and it seemed only right for him to apply those skills at a national level. His new role put him to work exploring, forming, and implementing partnerships in hundreds of cities, counties, and regions across America that involved denominational, ethnic, and racial diversity. The vision was to create sustained, holistic transformation wherever possible.

With Jarvis's departure, the board of Mission Mississippi began talking to me about the possibility of replacing him as the executive director. Needless to say, I devoted considerable prayer and soul-searching to their invitation. Unlike most of the other offers that had come my way, this opportunity was located right in the heart of Mississippi, only thirty miles up the road from where I grew up. Furthermore, it meant serving with leaders I knew well, in a cause I deeply believed in already. In my heart, I could sense that in Mission Mississippi, God was at last opening up a new door of ministry for me.

But what would be the best way for me to leave Mendenhall? I'd given almost thirty years of my life to the ministry there. Our home church was there. Many of my best friends were there. And of course my roots were there. With so many connections and factors involved, if I was going to do this, I wanted to leave in a way that would honor God and show respect to the other leaders in Mendenhall, yet still provide a clean break.

I had often seen other leaders do great damage when they left organizations they had founded or led for years. Sometimes they stomped off in a huff, rather than moving on in a peaceful and loving way. Other times they continued to influence things after their departure by exerting control from the side. I loved TMM too much to want to create any of those kinds of problems.

So I sought counsel from some friends in ministry who lived in Grand Rapids, Michigan. They made four recommendations: drop off the TMM board, stop serving as an elder at Mendenhall Bible Church, move out of Mendenhall, and change your church membership to another church.

I saw a lot of wisdom in all four suggestions. So Rosie and I determined to follow them, except for the fourth, changing our church membership. We loved Artis Fletcher and Tim Keyes and the people of MBC so much, and we felt that by retaining our church membership there, we could set an example of Christians graciously leaving a place while at the same time affirming our bond of fellowship. So ever since I left TMM, my family has continued to be active members of Mendenhall Bible Church, at least on Sundays.

When we moved up to the Jackson area, about an hour northwest of Mendenhall, we began attending New Horizon Church on Wednesday nights so our younger son, Ryan, could be part of the youth group there. For that reason, New Horizon's pastor, Ronnie Crudup, teased us as being his "Wednesday night members." But he and I became close friends.

I first met Ronnie before he was a pastor, when he was working with Entergy Power in Simpson County. He was the first black man to work with that company. They had courageously hired him in the days before it was considered acceptable to have a black in a position of responsibility.

One of Ronnie's cousins had been a member of Mendenhall Bible Church, so I had seen Ronnie at different occasions over the years.

After Ronnie entered the ministry, he became the pastor of a Baptist church in Jackson, and he invited me to speak there. That's when we really began to develop our friendship. He was also on the board of Mission Mississippi. So now that I was living in Jackson and attending New Horizon on Wednesdays, our relationship became quite close. I could tell he was a bright, up-and-coming leader in the Jackson area, a man with the potential to be the next Frank Pollard, a prominent man who had been the pastor of First Baptist Church and a major force for race relations in the 1980s and '90s. Ronnie's perception of the kingdom of God was so much larger than most people's. He never limited God's work to a denomination or a racial group but rather extended a "kingdom mentality" to anyone who was willing to serve the Lord.

Having realized that I didn't want to leave Mississippi, and having formulated a strategy for making a smooth transition out of Mendenhall, I wholeheartedly accepted the job as executive director of Mission Mississippi. In 1998, after traveling around the country preaching about racial reconciliation, it was a logical next step in my life's work. I saw this as an opportunity to speak into the lives of the Christian Church. Certainly, the major emphases of my time in Mendenhall had been evangelism and community development. But all of our ministry's efforts had been carried out against the backdrop of racism. Now, through Mission Mississippi, I along with another team of devoted fellow servants would be able to concentrate on bringing God's truth and grace to bear on that longstanding problem.

CHAPTER 5

The Sin of Silence

One of the biggest challenges in my work at Mission Mississippi is getting people to talk about racism and its effects. Obviously, issues of race can quickly become emotionally charged. For that reason, a lot of folks—both black and white—shy away from issues of race.

I myself had grown up in a black culture that taught us from the beginning to avoid racial topics at all costs. To engage in such a conversation was just asking for trouble. So black people learned how to say the "right" things to white people. They told white folks what they wanted to hear, not necessarily what the black folks honestly had to say. Blacks found that it was safer to keep smiling and joking and laughing, regardless of how they actually felt. That sort of behavior helped to keep the peace, but it also led to inauthentic relationships.

That's why when civil rights workers came to Mississippi in the 1960s to register black voters, they discovered that many blacks didn't want to sign up. At work, a white boss might ask the black employees, "Do you want to vote?" The blacks would reply, "No, Sir, we don't want to vote. Y'all white folks know how to run things better than we do, so you just take care of that." The registration workers had already heard of black employees losing their jobs if they registered to vote, so there was no way others would take that risk. It was safer to stay silent.

That happened a long time ago. Yet my own upbringing in that system still affects me to this day (although, praise God, I am much less affected by it now than I used to be). One time, when I was still heading up The Mendenhall Ministries, I was invited to meet with a white businessman whom I had identified as a potential donor. He welcomed me into his office, and we began to talk about my work. Then in the middle of the conversation, he asked me, "Dolphus, what do you think about affirmative action?"

A little warning light went off inside my mind. I found myself thinking, "Watch out! Be careful!" It was that same caution I had been raised to follow as a boy. I have to admit, for an instant I thought about playing it safe—what nowadays we call being "politically correct." After all, I had a ministry to run. I needed money to fund it.

Affirmative action was a side issue, largely unrelated to the core work of TMM. Why should I risk offending this man, who could be very helpful to what we were doing? He'd never know if I just told him what he wanted to hear (or rather, what I *assumed* he wanted to hear—although, on the other hand, it was possible that he was asking a trick question).

Praise God for speaking a different word into my heart that day: "Dolphus, how does being dishonest with this man serve My purposes? Which is more important—funding The Mendenhall

Ministries or seeking to build a bridge of understanding with this man, even if it feels risky?"

All of those thoughts and more went through my mind in the blink of an eye, although I'm sure I hesitated just long enough for the man to notice. Finally, I smiled and said, "Well, now, let me ask: do you want me to give you the answer I think you want to hear, or the answer I really believe?" He laughed, and we were able to have a frank conversation about a somewhat controversial subject. By God's grace, on that occasion, I triumphed over the sin of silence, a sin that had been nurtured in me from birth.

The Elephant in the Room

It's fair to say that Mission Mississippi exists as a direct response to the sin of silence. Our mission is "to encourage and demonstrate unity in the Body of Christ across racial and denominational lines so that communities throughout Mississippi can better understand the gospel message." That sounds like a worthwhile endeavor. But do you know how difficult it actually is to "encourage and demonstrate unity in the Body of Christ across racial and denominational lines"? It's difficult, in large part, because talking about issues of race is difficult for many, many people. Even people who are Christians.

I've mentioned some of the reasons why blacks back away from discussions about race. Their background tells them to run from danger. But whites also tend to avoid racial topics. Sometimes it may be that they sense a conflict is coming or that they will be put on the defensive. But all of the research shows that the number one reason whites don't talk about racism is that they think racism no longer exists.

In 2006, sociologist Lincoln Quillian of Northwestern University published an article that surveyed recent research on prejudice,

discrimination, and racism in the United States. He concluded that
except for a relatively few committed racists, "most white Americans
support the principle of equal treatment regardless of race and repu-
diate the practice of discrimination. At the same time, white [Amer-
icans] endorse many stereotypical beliefs, doubt the existence of
significant racial discrimination, and show low levels of support for
efforts to achieve racial equality through government intervention."[1]

Quillian's findings validate what I hear almost everywhere I go.
For more than thirty years, I have traveled extensively across the
United States, talking to folks about the gospel and the poor (especially the rural poor), and Christ's call to love, justice, and racial
reconciliation. For the most part, I've received overwhelming support, encouragement, and affirmation for my remarks whenever
I've spoken at predominantly white churches and other groups.

Nevertheless, the research Quillian cites is absolutely correct
about white people doubting that racial discrimination is still
a problem. "Racism is a thing of the past," I often hear. Another
comment is, "Yes, slavery and Jim Crow and lynchings and other
forms of racism happened in our nation's history. But those things
happened a long time ago. Things are different now. Thanks to the
Civil Rights Act, affirmative action, congressional redistricting,
and other developments, minorities have never had it better." Often
a person will add, "I'm certainly not a racist."

There's a lot I could say about those perceptions. But maybe the
comment that hurts the most is the one that goes, "Dolphus, it's
true that some terrible things have happened between the races in
our country's history. But we're beyond all that now. Yes, I know

---

1. Lincoln Quillian, "New Approaches to Understanding Racial Prejudice and
Discrimination," *Annual Review of Sociology* 32, no. 1 (August 2006): 299–328.

here and there things still happen, and people take offense. But can't we just deal with that and move on? Can't we just lighten up? Why do we have to keep focusing on racial issues? Doesn't that only make things worse?"

In other words, let's stay silent. Let's not talk about the elephant in the room. Let's just pretend that nothing is still wrong. If we don't talk about it, maybe it will go away. Will it? Has it? What do you see (or not see) when you look around at the people in your church at eleven o'clock on Sunday morning, let alone outside the church?

Indeed, for some white Americans, there exists a kind of racial ignorance, if you will. They actually believe that racism *has* gone away, because they don't consciously perceive it, nor are they aware of the many ways in which racial discrimination and bigotry still exist in our land. So to them, to talk about racism is to talk about a problem that doesn't exist.

But is that what the Bible encourages us to do—not to talk about racism? Hardly! The Bible teaches that silence in the face of any sin is itself a sin. James 4:17 says, "Anyone . . . who knows the good he ought to do and doesn't do it, sins." Likewise, passivity in the face of sin is never an option. Paul wrote, "Do not be overcome by evil, but overcome evil with good" (Rom. 12:21).

Throughout my ministry, I have challenged those of us who follow Christ to build bridges of reconciliation with people who don't look like us. In this chapter, I want to challenge us from the opposite direction—about what we *fail* to say and do.

You see, racism can be a sin of omission as well as commission. During the eighteenth and nineteenth centuries, the slave traders of England and other countries and the slave owners in the South could be said to have committed sins of commission, in that they knowingly, willingly, and actively practiced racism against

Africans. Meanwhile, many in England and many in the North shook their heads at those practices and said, in effect, "What a shame. That should not be." But they did nothing. In addition, most of them said nothing. They benefited from a racist system, but since they weren't directly involved in the slave trade, they acted as if slavery was someone else's problem. They didn't want to get involved. In that way, they practiced a sin of omission.

It may come as a shock to realize that anyone can be *passively* racist—whether black or white. "Who, *me?*" you may be thinking. "I'm certainly not a racist." No, maybe not actively. But when was the last time you laughed when someone told a racist joke? Or maybe you didn't laugh, but you also didn't speak up and challenge the inherent racism of the humor? When was the last time someone cut you off in traffic, and when you realized that the other driver was from another race or ethnic group, you had negative thoughts about that race or group? Suppose you're white: when was the last time you listened to a news report about some sad situation in a minority community and thought, "Well, of course that happened. Those people don't know how to live"? Or suppose you're black: when was the last time you heard about some white, corporate executive committing white-collar crime and thought, "Well, there you go! Isn't that just like those people"?

You don't have to be a member of a racist group to practice racism. You don't even have to feel prejudice against an entire race to practice racism. All you have to do is watch someone from another race being treated unjustly and remain silent.

Afraid to Speak Up

In the early 1960s, James Meredith, a man of both Native-American and African-American background, applied to the University of Mississippi. No African American had ever been admitted to that school. After Meredith's application was rejected twice, the NAACP (National Association for the Advancement of Colored People) filed suit on his behalf, charging that the only reason Meredith was being denied entry was the color of his skin. The case went all the way to the United States Supreme Court, which ruled that Meredith had the right to be admitted.

That set the stage for a showdown, and the governor of Mississippi at the time, a staunch segregationist named Ross Barnett, was only too pleased to accept the challenge. With Barnett's sponsorship, the state quickly passed a law prohibiting anyone who had been convicted of a "state crime" from being admitted to a state school. Meredith previously had been "convicted" of "false voter registration," which was a classic tactic used to deny black voters their right to vote.

Undeterred by the Mississippi law, Meredith attempted to enroll on September 20, 1962. He was turned back after Governor Barnett made a "triumphant" stand against blacks on the front steps of the university. US Attorney General Robert Kennedy then intervened and worked out a deal with the governor. On October 1, Meredith again tried to enroll, and this time was admitted. He was the first African American to attend Ole Miss.

The event touched off riots on campus in which two people were killed. US Marshals and troops from the US Army, Mississippi Army National Guard, and US Border Patrol were called in. Eventually, Meredith graduated from the University of Mississippi on August 18, 1963 with a degree in political science, yet throughout his time at the school, he was constantly harassed, insulted, and threatened by a handful of students who bitterly resented his presence. It's important to point out that the rest of the students at the university—all white—apparently had little if any problem with Meredith attending "their" school. At least they didn't voice their opposition, if they felt any. But they also didn't voice their support.

One member of that "silent majority" was Bill Morris.

In his heart, Bill was convinced that admitting James Meredith was the right thing for the school to do. At the same time, he feared that if he were to utter even one kind word to the new student who didn't look like him and everyone else, others would hear about it—and don't you know how difficult that could have made things for Bill! So Bill played it safe. He let fear rule his behavior. He kept his personal feelings about James Meredith coming to Ole Miss to himself.

It's interesting to think about what might have happened if Bill Morris had spoken up. Assuming that most of the white students felt as he did, he likely would have found far more support than opposition. In turn, what if even 5 or 10 percent of those support-ers had then spoken up? Could their intervention have turned the tide? Could their courage to stand up for James Meredith have ral-lied countless others to take a stand and make a statement that the days of segregation at Ole Miss were over? Could that "opposition to the opposition" have caused the governor and his supporters to stand down? Could it have prevented the riots, along with the senseless deaths of two people? Could their acceptance have trans-formed James's days at the University of Mississippi from a season of stress and tension to one of satisfying relationships and racial reconciliation?

We'll never know, because the many who supposedly were in favor of the black man remained silent, while the few who were unapologetically against him shouted hatred. In the end, whoever speaks the most and speaks the loudest tends to carry the day.

Who Is Our Neighbor?

I suppose most people would say that even if Bill Morris had shown more courage, he didn't actually do anything "wrong." But he himself didn't see it that way. For years after those events of the early 1960s, Bill secretly felt a lingering guilt for not having expressed kindness toward James Meredith at the very time when he needed it most. Finally, as Bill was watching a television interview of James Meredith, he saw a man wearing an Ole Miss hat talking about his love for the university. He saw no bitterness or anger in James Meredith's conversation, even when he was asked about the person who shot him during his historic march from Memphis to Jackson, a few years after he graduated from Ole Miss. When the program ended, Bill quickly called James Meredith and left a message on his voice mail, saying that he admired and appreciated him. When James called him back, they visited for well over an hour and agreed to get together.

Bill decided that Two and Two Day would be the right time and the right setting in which to express to James his remorse for remaining silent all those years ago. The idea behind Two and Two—an annual event sponsored by Mission Mississippi—is fairly simple: a black couple and a white couple share a meal at a local restaurant, two and two. By doing so, a number of valuable things take place. First, two couples have an opportunity to get to know people who don't look like them. The hope is to promote productive dialogue, greater understanding, and ultimately, racial reconciliation. Another outcome is to show everyone who sees those couples dining together that blacks and whites can reach across racial lines to socialize and form relationships. The message is, it's okay to mingle. And of course, it never hurts to stimulate the local economy by getting people out to eat.

When they got together for Two and Two Day, James accepted Bill's apology and forgave him. While they ate, Bill recounted his college experience, and described how he had felt when James was finally admitted to Ole Miss. Then he recalled how he had let fear keep him from pursuing a friendship with James while they were students. Bill told James that night, while the couples were dining, that he had not only won freedom for his race, but also for everyone else who was unknowingly a prisoner of the system of segregation. The evening opened the door to what became a great friendship.

Bill Morris's story is instructive on many levels. But one of the main things it shows is that the sin of silence is usually committed by people who generally are "on our side," people we otherwise regard as friends, not enemies, because they are not doing anything against us. Thus their unwillingness to speak up when we need them most feels like a kind of betrayal.

Recall Jesus' parable of the Good Samaritan. Jesus told that story in response to a scholar of the Mosaic Law who tested him by asking, in effect, "When the Law tells me to love my neighbor as myself, who is my neighbor?" Most of us would think of a "neighbor" as someone like us, someone who is generally on our side, someone who acts toward us in a friendly manner, someone who cares.

So Jesus begins the parable with the words, "A certain man," meaning a certain Jewish man. He wants to make the point that this man is not unlike the legal scholar. He is a Jew. He is one of the scholar's own. In effect, he and the scholar are neighbors. Jesus tells how the man is robbed, beaten, and left for dead in the middle of the road. Soon a priest comes by—again, a Jew, just like the beaten man, and a man whose occupation is very much aligned with the lawyer's. But despite the ethnic bond, "he passed by on the other side." Likewise a Levite—also a Jew and a religious figure—comes upon the crime scene. He also "passed by on the other side."

Jesus doesn't tell us what is in the minds of these two travelers, but He doesn't have to. Clearly, they don't want to get involved. "It's not my problem. Someone else can deal with this."

Then a Samaritan comes along, a man from an ethnic group that was despised by the priest, the Levite, and even by the wounded man himself. And of course he was despised by that legal scholar too. But this man goes out of his way to attend to the wounded man's needs, prompting the clincher of a question, "Which of these three do you think proved to be a neighbor to the man who fell into the robbers' hands?" (Luke 10:25–37 NASB).

Again, the sin of silence tends to be committed by people we would otherwise think are "on our side."

Indifference Rather Than Making a Difference

I experienced a form of this sin of silence while serving as the executive director of The Mendenhall Ministries. I was often invited to speak to churches and other groups of Christians throughout Mississippi and elsewhere. I invariably talked about the gospel, about Christ's love for all people, culminating in His sacrificial, atoning death on the cross. I also talked about Christ's love extending to the poor, and particularly to the rural poor. I showed how the gospel has both spiritual and material implications, as evidenced by Jesus' words and work among the poor of His day. I used TMM as a model for how Christians can bring the gospel to poor people in our day.

Naturally, I hoped that some of those who listened to my messages would get behind TMM and support us through prayer, funding, and sending volunteers. After all, these were fellow Christians, brothers and sisters in Christ—neighbors! But to my surprise—and disappointment—not very many conservative churches would contribute to our work. They liked the fact that we "preached the gospel," which to them meant calling people to repentance from sin and putting faith in Christ as their Savior. But beyond that, they were not interested in helping. They considered the health clinic, the law office, the farm, the tutoring programs, the Genesis One school, and all the other things we were doing as somehow outside the scope of what the church ought to be involved with. "We only want to support the preaching of the gospel," they would say. But they remained silent about poor people's material needs. In that way, they followed the priest and the Levite in the parable: confronted with desperate physical needs, they simply "passed by on the other side."

Other churches remained silent—and racist—in a rather passive-aggressive way. Most of those churches were nearby in Mississippi, where strict segregation had been practiced for generations. They just didn't want to see things improve for black people. They never said that out loud. But they practically shouted it from the rooftops by what they *didn't* say. Oh, they thought it was fine to preach salvation to black people, and even to tell black folk that they too were "created in the image of God." But now, let's not go so far as to tell them that they could vote or go to college, or become a police chief or a doctor or a banker or whatever, or otherwise enjoy the rights of a "full" citizen.

As I say, they never exactly said those things publicly. Only an out-and-out racist would do that (or so they likely believed). No, they kept their mouths shut but their inaction seemed to show that they harbored those thoughts in their hearts. That kind of silence was deafening! Especially at a time when blacks needed the support of white Christians more than ever.

That unspoken prejudice was sourced, as it usually is, in fear—fear that if Dolphus and his coworkers at TMM started encouraging black people to grow beyond their history and embrace what the United States Constitution said were simply their rights as citizens, then the culture would be turned upside down in ways no one was prepared for. So they wanted to keep the black churches passive, places where souls could be saved for eternity but people's present circumstances would in no way be affected.

I really believe that churches and groups like that are in the minority in the body of Christ today. But what difference does it make if the other churches, the ones that form the majority, sit on the sidelines and do nothing? Prejudice thrives on indifference.

The Power and Pain of a Symbol

I saw that truth firsthand in 2001 when, at the invitation of Governor Ronnie Musgrove, I served on the Mississippi State Flag Commission. The commission was established to consider a new flag for our state. The Mississippi Supreme Court had ruled that the original state flag, adopted in 1894, was technically not legitimate. That flag had been rejected by the state legislature in 1906, but the state never adopted a different flag. And so the 1894 flag continued to be used, though unofficially.

The traditional flag was offensive to many in that it incorporated the "stars and bars" of the Confederacy's battle flag. Needless to say, that design has always been painful for most African Americans in our state, because it is too closely identified with the terrible history of racism, both before and since the Civil War. However, many white citizens take pride in their Confederate roots, and they regarded the 1894 flag as a worthy symbol of their heritage.

The seventeen-member commission, chaired by former governor

William Winter, was tasked with designing a new flag that would unite everyone in the state around a shared vision. The new design would compete against the traditional design, and whichever flag won would become the official state flag.

We met for about six sessions to hear a variety of views and opinions from people across the state. Then we went to work on designing a new flag. We ended up with a flag that kept the same color scheme and layout as the old flag, except that the "stars and bars" were replaced by a blue canton with twenty, five-pointed stars: nineteen small white stars surrounding one large white star. The outer ring of thirteen stars represented the original thirteen colonies of the United States, and the inner ring of six stars represented the six nations that had sovereignty over Mississippi territory during its history. Together the nineteen small stars of the rings also represented the number of states that were already part of the Union when Mississippi joined in 1817. The innermost star, larger than the rest, represented Mississippi itself.

I thought it was a beautiful design, and the members of our commission were convinced that it represented our state very well. They were hopeful that all Mississippians would be proud to identify themselves with this new flag. They especially hoped that the conflicts over the traditional flag would be left behind.

But it was not to be. Since the issue was so controversial, the legislature opted not to vote on it, but instead to add the flag decision as a referendum on the popular ballot, so that the people of Mississippi could vote on it. When the votes were tallied, the 1894 flag was adopted by 65 percent, compared to 35 percent for the new flag. As a result, the traditional design, with its Confederate symbol, is now our official state flag.

I respected the results of that vote, but I was deeply disappointed.

I had been so excited about the new design and felt that it represented all of the people of Mississippi much better than the old design. I had two particular hopes riding on the outcome of the vote. First, I had hoped that voting in a new flag would show the rest of the country that a state with an ugly history of racism can change and become unified around something positive that represents all of its people. That didn't happen. As a result, I'm sure that many Americans saw the vote and thought, "Well, of course Mississippi would keep a flag with racist overtones."

My second hope was that the Christian community would support the new design. But the fact that only 35 percent of voters voted for it suggests that most of the Christians in our state by and large sided with the traditionalists.

I now have a new appreciation for why that happened. You see, blacks and whites who grew up in Mississippi in the 1940s, '50s, and '60s grew up in two separate worlds—two very different worlds—with the result that the old flag means different things to each group. Many of my white friends grew up in a world that emphasized Mississippi's grand old traditions, natural beauty, sense of honor, and Southern charm. To them, the old flag symbolizes everything they love about our state. Doing away with that symbol would feel like repudiating all of the best things that Mississippi stands for.

Black folks, however, have had a very different experience. Regardless of how we may feel today, Mississippi in the 1940s, '50s, and '60s was not a place we wanted to preserve; it was a place we desperately wanted to leave. So when we look at the old flag, we tend to see a symbol of shame, not pride. To us that flag symbolizes every racial injustice that was ever committed against black people.

I've come to realize that both experiences—and both perspectives—must be respected. So I've made peace with the outcome of the vote. And I'm learning to see the old flag in some new ways by trying to look at it through the eyes of my white brothers and sisters.

Of course, I remain keen on helping my white brothers and sisters appreciate the pain that many black Mississippians feel whenever they look at that flag. I believe that followers of Christ are called to pay attention to such matters. Indeed, the New Testament makes it clear that Christians are to do nothing that offends another brother or sister in Christ. Paul wrote, "Let us . . . determine this—not to put an obstacle or a stumbling block in a brother's way. . . . It is good not . . . to do anything by which your brother stumbles" (Rom. 14:13, 21 NASB).

My hope had been that the Christians in our state would use the flag decision as an opportunity to come together and say, "If our brothers and sisters in Christ are offended by the old flag, then we need to do away with that flag and create a new flag that represents all of us from this time on." For the reasons I've noted, that did not happened. So be it. But I still wonder, was support for a flag that many find offensive really the message that Christians wanted to communicate? Could embracing such a flag affect the way that black Mississippians listen and respond when Christians talk about Christ's love?

As I say, I was deeply disappointed that my two hopes were not realized. But I did walk away from the state flag commission with a much clearer idea of why Mission Mississippi is needed in our state. There are still so many lingering racial tensions that need to be dealt with and overcome. I realized that it's not enough to just settle for "putting up with" people who are different from us. Rather, we've got to actively learn how to have genuine concern for all people.

Another result of that experience was that I learned to be a better listener to people who are different from me. Those who testified before the commission came from all kinds of backgrounds and perspectives, and they presented remarkably different ideas, often very passionately. Sitting through those sessions helped me learn to really hear what people were saying, and to appreciate their points of view and the reasoning behind their thinking, even when I felt that their conclusions were wrong. In the end, the voters chose to adopt a flag that 65 percent of Mississippians can look at and say, "That's my flag." But not all of us can say that. I will always wonder if that outcome came about because a lot of people didn't speak up about a controversial but very significant issue.

A Voice of Authority

So what happens if someone does speak up in the face of injustice and prejudice? Thankfully, we have some great models to follow in people who have taken bold stands to promote genuine reconciliation between whites and blacks. One of the most outstanding was my friend, the late Dr. Frank E. Pollard, former pastor of First Baptist Church in Jackson. Dr. Pollard, a white pastor in a white church, was willing to "push the buttons" on racial matters at a time when it was unpopular and risky to do so.

A man of great humility as well as great strength and conviction, Dr. Pollard spent years nudging his congregation forward in dealing with their attitudes toward African Americans. He knew all too well that his church had been known historically as a bastion of segregation. So he began preaching on racial reconciliation based on the gospel, challenging his people to think and act differently from what their Southern heritage had taught them. (Dr. Pollard's effectiveness in the pulpit was praised in 1979 when *Time* magazine cited him as one of the seven best preachers in America.[2]) He also recognized that he would have to lead by example, so he skillfully orchestrated symbolic gestures that signaled to his congregation that he was serious about what he was saying. For example, he arranged for the Rev. E. V. Hill, pastor of Mt. Zion Missionary Baptist Church in Los Angeles, to speak at First Baptist for a Sunday evening service. Later he paved the way for Dr. Tony Evans, pastor of Oak Cliff Bible Fellowship in Dallas and head of The Urban Alternative, to address a statewide denominational convention.

Dr. Pollard's gracious but tenacious leadership also extended to me. In April 1998, three months into my role as executive director of Mission Mississippi, I spoke at a prayer breakfast in Jackson on the topic of building bridges of reconciliation. Dr. Pollard, who was also on the program that day, approached me right after I finished my remarks and said, "Dolphus, I want you to consider giving that same message at First Baptist, Jackson." I was stunned by the offer, but I was so excited that I accepted on the spot. He was excited as well, although he told me it would take a while to actually work me into the church's preaching schedule.

A month or two later, Dr. Pollard called me back. "Dolphus, the board has approved for you to speak," he said. "But now, I need to make you aware of something first. You will be the first African American ever to preach from our pulpit on a Sunday morning. In fact, we've never had a black man stand in the pulpit on Sunday morning. Are you okay with that?"

I told him I understood and that I had no problem with it. But in my heart, I started feeling pretty nervous and overwhelmed at

2. "Religion: American Preaching: A Dying Art?" *Time*, December 31, 1979, http://www.time.com/time/magazine/article/0,9171,912616,00.html.

the thought of being the first African American to stand in that historic pulpit on a Sunday morning. I could begin to appreciate, in just a small way, what James Meredith must have felt as he contemplated enrolling as the first black student at the University of Mississippi. It's exciting to get to be the one who finally breaks through a racial barrier. But the enormity of what that means—the legacy of the past, the expectations to perform and whether I'd be "good enough," the awareness that some in the congregation might prefer that I had *not* been invited to preach, and the challenge of what to say and how to say it—all of that and more clutched at my heart as I spent the next few months preparing for First Baptist of Jackson.

The Sunday morning finally arrived in November. I got up at about 4:00 AM to review my notes and make final preparations to preach. But as I was looking over my material, I found tears filling my eyes, and felt a deep, deep sadness. I began crying out in prayer, "Lord, I can preach this in California, I can preach this in Denver, I can preach this in New York—but Lord, I can't preach this in Jackson, Mississippi!" Deep pain was welling up in me because of how difficult I perceived the task.

I was remembering stories I'd heard from the past about white people standing at the door of First Baptist of Jackson, telling black people they weren't welcome; they couldn't come in. Even though I knew in my mind that those people and those events were long gone, in my heart I couldn't understand how that same church could now be ready for me to preach there—and to preach about racial reconciliation, no less! This was a real breakthrough opportunity, no doubt about it. But it was a very fearful moment for me, and I pleaded with God to give me the strength and courage I would need.

Of course God did exactly that. He used Dr. Pollard to help me feel totally welcome from the moment I arrived at the church. I preached both the 9:00 AM and 11:00 AM services. After both of them, members of the congregation formed long lines to greet me enthusiastically with hugs, handshakes, and words of kindness that expressed great appreciation for my message. As I took in their words, I realized that their hearts had been prepared to hear what I had to say. They wanted a way to articulate their desire to turn away from the past and begin embracing black folks with the love of Christ. They truly wanted that, but they had been boxed up in silence. My presence that morning enabled them to start talking.

So it was a breakthrough Sunday for what God was accomplishing at First Baptist through Dr. Pollard's leadership. It was also a breakthrough Sunday for what God was accomplishing in Dolphus Weary. I was so grateful for the response and the openness of those people—people who didn't look like me—to God's Word about a very sensitive subject. And I was just thrilled beyond words that God would choose to use me in such a wonderful way. Once again, I experienced that strange feeling of "What am *I* doing here?"

A few days later, I had occasion to stop back by First Baptist. While I was there, one of the custodians came up to me in a hallway. He was an elderly black man. He looked me in the eye and said, "Thank you for speaking at this church. I was here that day, and I never dreamed that a black man would ever speak from the pulpit of First Baptist Church." What a joy and encouragement that was! Such a confirmation that the gospel has the power to bridge the divide that separates one race from another.

That Sunday at First Baptist was probably the most significant opportunity I've ever had to preach across racial lines. It was certainly the most emotional for me. But there have been many other exciting moments as well, such as the Sunday night later in 1998 when I was invited to preach at the historic First Presbyterian Church in Jackson, also an all-white church. I've also been honored to speak to scores of other churches, rallies, conferences, men's gatherings, Christian colleges and universities, and in other settings all across the country. Many of them have been predominantly white.

Whenever I speak to my white brothers and sisters in Christ, my intent is not to "go get 'em," as a few people have encouraged me to do, in the belief that my African-American heritage gives me the right to "speak truth to power" and lecture the white man on changing his ways. That's never been my style. Rather, I simply want to share what the love of Christ has done in *my* life so as to inspire people with hope about what the love of Christ can do in their lives. And yes, that includes racial reconciliation. Sometimes talking about that makes everyone uncomfortable. And sometimes talking about that means talking openly about some hard truths and realities. But the point should never be about "going after" anybody, but about helping the body of Christ grow beyond racial divisions so all of us can become more Christlike, which means becoming the very best that God intends for us to be.

That has been the philosophy and heartbeat of Mission Mississippi, and that's why its work is so critically important. You see, the reason people remain silent on difficult issues is because no one is taking leadership to start the conversation. By actively, intentionally, and creatively getting blacks and whites together to pray, talk, eat, socialize, and work together as the body of Christ, Mission Mississippi is facilitating the conversation.

We desperately need that conversation! We need it in order to overcome the fear in our own hearts about people who don't look like us. We also need it in order to help the people who don't look like us overcome their fears about us. And we most especially need it in order to drown out those other voices—which, it turns out, are just a small but vocal minority of folks—that spew out words of hate, prejudice, malice, misunderstanding, misinformation, suspicion, division, and judgment. It's all too easy to let their evil words carry the day by retreating into silence. But if we'll engage in open dialogue about what we share as brothers and sisters in Christ, we won't have to be overcome by that evil. Instead we can overcome evil with good (Rom. 12:21).

CHAPTER 6

The Power of Parenting

No family is ever perfect, primarily because no person is perfect (except Jesus). So there have been lots of lessons that I've had to learn about family life. Many of the lessons I learned growing up have significantly impacted my family life today as well as my ministry. And all that Rosie and I and our family have been through since she and I married has played a profound role in shaping me into who I am today.

The family I grew up in was the product of five different marriages. Both my mother and my father had been married previously, and they had had children before they were married to each other. All together, they had six children between them. When I was four years old, my father left one day and abandoned us. Both he and my mother eventually remarried and had additional children with their new spouses. So, counting all of my full siblings and stepsiblings, there were twenty-one of us.

Not that we ever lived together all in one place. The only family that I ever really lived with consisted of my mother, seven of my brothers and sisters, and me. My father was pretty much a non-entity in my life, because of the way he took off on us. That placed untold demands on my mother to raise eight children by herself. Her situation prevented her from having a very close relationship with any of us. But I was in awe of her commitment to seeing that all of our needs were met, that we got as good an education as we possibly could, and that her children would be raised in a moral and Christ-honoring way.

That was my background going into my marriage to Rosie. Needless to say, I had to learn how to be a husband, and later how to be a father. Really, I had to learn how to be a man, since no one had ever modeled that for me when I was a boy. I certainly was able to look back at the situation I grew up in and determine that I wanted something very different for my own marriage and for my children. But I didn't have much to go on as far as how to be that different kind of husband and father.

My Magnificent Mate

However, one thing I did have going for me was that when Rosie and I got married, we both felt a strong conviction to make our marriage work, and to stick together "until death do us part." I had come from a broken family, and neither of us wanted to have to endure that, nor could we imagine putting our children through that kind of painful experience. So for us, divorce was never an option. We were committed to making our marriage work.

Of course, the best thing I had going for me was Rosie herself. In Rosie, God gave me an incredible blessing. She has been a magnificent partner throughout our marriage, both at home and in the various ministries God has allowed us to have. We decided early on that Rosie and I would work together in whatever things God brought our way so we could share every aspect of our lives and, as much as possible, limit the time we would have to spend apart.

So during our days at The Mendenhall Ministries, Rosie filled a variety of roles, wherever she was needed most. Early on, she served as secretary for John Perkins and me. As the ministry began to grow and we added a health clinic, we needed a receptionist at that new facility, and Rosie stepped into that position. Soon after, the health clinic developed a community health education program, which needed someone to go into the schools and share health tips with students. Rosie then became a community health education worker. Later, when we needed a nurse's aid at the clinic, Rosie pursued training and took on that job. At one point she served as the secretary for Artis Fletcher, the pastor of Mendenhall Bible Church, and then at TMM again as a secretary for me and travel coordinator.

Clearly, Rosie has lived out her faith in a beautiful way by taking the role of a servant in so many different areas. Through it all, she has been indispensable to my life. She is truly my mentor, my model, and especially my prayer warrior. She gets up every morning at about 4:30 or 5:00 and spends an hour or two reading the Bible and praying. That sets a high standard for me, because one of my weaknesses is that I don't always spend nearly enough time alone with the Lord each day. In that way, Rosie serves as a kind of spiritual buffer in my life, by continually lifting me up in prayer, but also by challenging me to a higher level. Frequently, she'll ask, "Dolphus, are you spending time with the Lord like you need to?" What a blessing to have a wife who is so intentional about building me up spiritually! Without question, Rosie has been my soul mate and partner in anything I've ever done that mattered.

The Girl with a Dream

Our oldest child and only daughter is Danita. She was born in April 1974, one week after a terrible flood in Mendenhall. (The Black Quarters, as our part of Mendenhall was called, sits in a low-lying area next to a creek that for years would flood annually, driving people out of their homes, and yet for some reason the county never could seem to find the money to build a flood-control system for that part of town.)

Growing up, Danita certainly felt the pains of racism. She learned early on what it meant to live on "our side" of the railroad tracks, in the Quarters. She also experienced prejudice when she went to junior high and high school—ironically, more of it from the teachers and administrators than from her fellow classmates. Danita was one of the smartest kids at her high school, but being black, she paid a price for that. It seemed as if the school was doing everything it could to keep her from graduating at the top of her class. No one wanted a black girl to out do any of the white students. But in the end, her grades were so good and her accomplishments so great that they had no choice but to honor her as first in her class.

One particularly bothersome conversation took place with the guidance counselor as she was entering her freshman year. By then, Danita had already won numerous awards, and she had consistently maintained one of the highest grade-point averages in middle school. But the counselor emphatically tried to steer her toward a set of classes aimed at preparing her for a vocational career, rather than toward a college preparatory curriculum. Meanwhile, that same counselor had advised many of Danita's white classmates to take college prep courses, even though most of them were making lower grades than Danita. That greatly frustrated Danita, because she had every intention—as well as the grades and the drive—to go on to college.

Truth be told, Danita has always had very high aspirations for her life. And she's always done whatever it takes to follow through on her dreams. Her dream for her career was birthed while we were living in Mendenhall. She saw firsthand the health clinic come into existence and noticed what a difference it immediately started to make in the community. She was able to observe and interact with Dr. Dennis Adams, the Christian doctor who practiced there. He was the first black doctor in Simpson County. I believe the model of Dr. Adams, more than anything else, helped Danita realize that no matter how challenging the circumstances might be for a young black girl growing up in Mississippi, it was still possible to become a doctor, if that's what she wanted to do and was willing to work for it. So that's precisely what she set out to do—no matter what the guidance counselor might say!

Among the colleges that Danita began considering was Rhodes College in Memphis, Tennessee. We went to visit the campus with her and were immediately struck by how beautiful the buildings and grounds were. But that's where the grinding poverty of my childhood began to come back and haunt me. "We probably can't afford to send our daughter here," I started thinking. "There's no way we have enough money to get Danita into a school like this." Do you see how poverty creates a mind-set? It causes a person to look at every financial decision and think, "I can't afford that," instead of thinking more hopefully and creatively, "*How* can I afford that? *How* can I make that happen?" Here I was, a grown man, and someone who had seen God provide amazing sums of money in amazing ways. But I was going back to that mind-set of poverty, which is so hard to break.

And if I doubted we could afford Rhodes while we were walking around the campus, my doubts were confirmed when the people at the financial aid office told us it would probably cost our family about $20,000 a year for Danita to attend. "Well, that's that," I concluded, quickly losing all hope. I was disappointed for Danita, because I knew she really had her heart set on Rhodes. But all was not lost. She had already received a full-tuition scholarship from another school up in the Midwest. So we began to focus on that possibility instead.

However, I guess Danita's faith in God's ability to provide was a lot stronger than mine, as was her clarity and insistence about the school she needed to attend. All along she had been praying for a college that would prepare her for medical school. She wanted that school to be outside of Mississippi, but not too far away from her family. Rhodes would be an ideal place on all counts.

Meanwhile, Rosie was also praying from the perspective of a mother. So perhaps it was her prayers that the Lord ultimately decided to grant. At any rate, two weeks after our visit to Rhodes we received a letter from the school explaining that Danita had been accepted for admission. It went on to say that because of her outstanding academic record in high school, Rhodes was giving her an academic scholarship package that would cover all but about $1,000 a year. That we could afford! So we had quite a time rejoicing over the news, recognizing that God had providentially been at work to bring Danita one important step closer to her dream.

That fall, we took Danita to Memphis and got her settled into her new school. As Rosie and I drove home on Interstate 55, tears filled my eyes. My mind was pondering what it really meant for us to have a daughter at a school like Rhodes. When I was growing up, college was something most black teenagers would never even consider. And if they did manage to get into a college, it wouldn't be at an expensive private school like Rhodes. I also thought about the expectations Danita had had to overcome. She was from a small school in a tiny rural town. That and the fact that she was an African American would tend to cause many people to assume she couldn't be academically prepared for college, let alone for a school like Rhodes. Certainly, her high school guidance counselor had said as much. But Danita had proven all the naysayers wrong by earning top grades and scores and by winning a valuable scholarship as a result. I felt so proud of her!

After graduating from Rhodes, Danita decided to attend the University of Tennessee College of Medicine, also in Memphis. Rosie and I were concerned about where she would live, but again, God showed us that He was at work in Danita's life. While she was at Rhodes, Danita had often been a babysitter for the nine-year-old daughter of a couple who were both doctors. They were so pleased with the model Danita had set for their child that when they learned she would be staying in Memphis for medical school, they offered to take care of her living arrangements if she would continue to babysit for their daughter. The apartment she ended up in was in a very nice neighborhood a mere five blocks away from the school. What a blessing from the Lord!

Danita had dared to start dreaming a fairly specific dream when she was in high school, and to that end she had started praying a fairly specific prayer: "Lord, I want You to allow me to become a Christian physician so I can use my gifts and training to help children." And on the strength of that, she chased her dream. After graduating from med school, she went to the University of South Alabama Medical Center, in Mobile, and in June 2003 completed her residency in pediatrics. Today she lives in Natchez, Mississippi, where she's serving children with her medical skills.

Needless to say, Rosie and I are extremely proud of our daughter and of her hard and faithful work to become a doctor—the first doctor in the Weary family! We can't wait to see the ways that God will continue to use her in the future.

Struggling to Make His Way

Our second child, Reggie, was born on July 16, 1976. When he was seven, Reggie was diagnosed with a form of cancer called non-Hodgkins lymphoma, which attacks the lymph nodes. That development brought us to a screeching halt—and sent us to our knees in prayer.

For a long time I found myself praying the question, "Why Lord? Why does one of my children have to go through something like this? Why does he have to endure the pain of chemo treatments? Why does he have to live with the fear of wondering whether he'll live to be an adult? Why is this happening to me and to my family? Here I am, involved in ministry, trying to serve You, trying to bring Your love to this community. I came back to Mississippi, just like You asked me. Why does this have to happen to me? Why is it happening to my son?"

I prayed those questions for a while, but then God began to lead Rosie to challenge me with a different question: "Why *not* us, Dolphus? Why *not* our family? What right do we have to be excused from the kind of tests and challenges that everyone else goes through? Can we trust the Lord even if we have to walk through the valley of the shadow of death?" It was liberating to start realizing that God was with us as a family no matter what. And so we just put it all in His hands. Thankfully, He allowed Reggie's cancer to go into remission.

I believe Reggie struggled growing up as the second child, especially when his older sister was seemingly All-Everything in high school. She was academically inclined, while he was more interested in sports. Reggie worked hard in school, but he never quite made the kind of grades that Danita was able to make. I know he also struggled as the son of a charismatic leader in the community, because people were always comparing him to me in one way or another. The fact that my work had to do with racial reconciliation no doubt put added pressure on him, because how he related to any white person would always reflect one way or another on me. Adding all of that up, Reggie struggled to find his own unique identity, distinct from his parents who were the "spiritual leaders" and from his sister who was the aspiring doctor.

The effects of racism also had a profound impact on Reggie. One time I rented the movie *Amistad*, the Steven Spielberg film about a mutiny aboard a slave ship in the early 1800s. I tried to get Reggie to watch it, believing that it would be a valuable way to help him come to grips with his roots. But he just could not. "There's just too much pain," he told me.

I remember the challenges Reggie experienced in being the only black on his high school's tennis team. He would come home and describe the feelings of resentment that some of the white boys on the team expressed toward him, along the lines of, "Why are you here? Why are you playing tennis? We let y'all play basketball. We let y'all play football. Why can't you black kids be satisfied with those sports? Why do you have to come over here to tennis now and invade the white people's game?" (Never mind African-American tennis stars like Arthur Ashe, who won three Grand Slam titles, or Althea Gibson, who won multiple Wimbledon women's titles in both singles and doubles, not to mention other more recent champions.)

Reggie managed to stand strong and make it through high

school. After graduating, he applied to Tougaloo College in Jackson, a historic African-American school, because he had a number of friends who had gone there. Rosie and I were all for that, and we were as thrilled when he got accepted as we had been when Danita was accepted into Rhodes. We thought he might even play on the basketball team, since in high school he had been a starting point guard during his senior year. But Reggie had gotten burned out on basketball, thanks to an overly aggressive coach who thought the way to motivate players was to yell at them, grab them, shake them, call them names, and otherwise instill fear. All that did for Reggie was to make him never want to play organized basketball again.

That was so unfortunate, because I can recall how beneficial basketball had been for me as a young man. It helped give my life focus and direction. It also gave me confidence. Reggie could have used a lot of that, because as he entered college, he began struggling in his Christian walk. It wasn't that he was getting into trouble. But he was drifting in his relationship with the Lord. As much as anything, I think he was trying to figure out who Reggie was.

Naturally, that affected his studying and caused his grades to suffer. When he found out that he wasn't going to graduate in four years, or maybe even in five years, he wanted to drop out of school. But Rosie strongly encouraged him to hang in there and graduate. To say that we as parents were very concerned with what might happen if our son quit college would be an understatement: there was no way we were going to let him *not* graduate! So what an exciting day it was when he walked across the stage to receive his bachelor of science degree from Tougaloo.

We had another scare, though, in early 1999, while he was still attending college. One day he found a lump on his thyroid, and naturally we thought that his childhood cancer was coming back.

Once again we cried out to God in prayer (not like we hadn't been praying for Reggie day and night all along). Thanks to Danita, who was attending medical school at that time, we were able to locate just the right doctor at the University of Mississippi Medical Center in Jackson. Reggie had to have surgery to remove his thyroid. But thankfully his voice was not affected, and he quickly returned to full health.

Twists and Turns

After graduating, Reggie went to work at a new wireless phone company called SunCom. It was a great job, and he was doing well in it. But soon it became evident that Reggie was going through a number of changes. He was still struggling in terms of his identity. He was also trying to fit in to a new job and a new living situation, with new friends and acquaintances. Unfortunately, he did not establish a strong base of support and reinforcement, and in trying to find himself, he got involved with people who were not a good influence.

Reggie was not out of God's grasp, however. On one occasion he went to New Orleans with a friend. It was late at night as they were driving back, and he was feeling sleepy. They decided to pull off the highway and catch some sleep. But it was too late. As they cruised down a side road to find a place to stop, Reggie began falling asleep at the wheel. He came to just as the car went flying off the pavement and into a lake. Just as they hit the water, he thought to push the button that opened the window, so they could climb out of the car. They managed to scramble their way onto the top of the car. It was 2:30 in the morning.

Looking back on it later, Reggie felt that God chose that moment to provide a miracle. The road they drove off of had been utterly deserted, and now they were stuck in a lake in the middle of nowhere, on top of a sinking car, covered by the dark of night. Then suddenly someone was calling out to them, asking if they were all right. Reggie began shouting for help. The person yelled back that he was contacting the sheriff. Soon aid arrived, and before long Reggie and his friend were safely on land. After the car got pulled out of the water and towed away, they rode with the sheriff to the precinct office to make a statement. Reggie never saw or found out who it was that had called out to them in the dark. "Dad," he told me later, "it must have been God sending an angel." We all looked on it as the Lord sparing Reggie's life.

Not long after that incident, the men's movement Promise Keepers held a gathering in Jackson. I was a cochair for the event, and I invited Reggie to come with me to the rally. In response to the speakers' challenge to us as men to humble ourselves before God and to live our lives to His glory and by His strength, my son rededicated his life to Christ, committing himself to start walking with the Lord once again. What I had been unable to do as a father, our Heavenly Father had done. I was so thankful. And hopeful.

On January 1, 2004, the Weary family sat down to our annual New Year's dinner. We've made that meal a tradition, using it as a time to look back over the previous year and recount the blessings God has given us and the lessons learned, and then to talk about the challenges, joys, and hopes for the year to come. Danita shared enthusiastically about her new work as a doctor. Our younger son Ryan (more on him to come) talked about his hopes for the coming year. Then it was Reggie's turn. He stunned us with something we didn't want to hear: his girlfriend was expecting his baby.

In retrospect, maybe we as a family should have found some way to celebrate the fact that a new life was coming into this world—a new member of the Weary family, and the first grandchild. But that didn't happen. New Year's dinner was more or less over at that point. The shock was just too great. It took me at least a month to get over it. Fortunately, it took Rosie a lot less time than that. Very quickly she moved alongside Reggie and his girlfriend with support and help, adopting the attitude, "This is our son. We need to move forward."

I was a lot slower in accepting the situation. After all, hadn't God spared Reggie's life—not once but multiple times? Hadn't I experienced the thrill of watching Reggie rededicate his life to Christ at the Promise Keepers rally? And now this. This was not what I wanted. Surely this could not be what God wanted.

But as I cried out to God for wisdom as to how to make sense of the situation, He led me to 2 Samuel 12, which tells what happened after David fathered a child by Uriah's wife, Bathsheba. The infant became ill, and David fasted and prayed for the baby to recover. But the child died anyway. When David realized that his son was no longer alive, the text says he washed himself, worshipped the Lord, and then went on with his life. What I realized from that Scripture was that I had to start dealing with the reality of the situation. I had to get past the issue of what I wanted, or even of what God might have wanted, and start dealing with the reality of what was going to be. "This is my son," I thought to myself. "A grandchild is going to be born. My not liking the way this is coming about is immaterial to reality. Wash up, clean up, and move on." So I did. The initial shock of Reggie's news went away.

I made it a point to start helping Reggie save money and get out of debt, because he said he wanted to buy a house. Frankly, I was concerned whether he would even be able to rent an apartment. So I began working with him to form the practice of saving $500 a month minimum. "Reggie," I told him, "if you can show that you can save $500 a month over time, you can prove that you're able to rent an apartment." He began doing that. Then he found a house that he really wanted to buy. I went with him to look at the house, and it looked like something that might work. So I encouraged him, "Take a couple more months to work on this. Keep doing what you're doing."

The Phone Call

On the Friday in June before Father's Day, I was out in the yard laying some grass sod. Reggie came out and helped me, even though he was getting ready to leave on a brief trip over the weekend. On Monday he returned, but Rosie and I had already gone down to Baton Rouge for a speaking engagement.

When we got home on Wednesday, I found a shirt laid out on my bed with a note that read, "Happy Belated Father's Day." That was Reggie's gift to me for Father's Day. Later that evening, he called. We had a good conversation, talking about his trip and his plans and things in general. Then we said good-bye, and Rosie and I went to bed.

Less than an hour later, the phone rang. It was that call that every parent dreads: accident, son in the hospital, come immediately, yes, I understand, click. And then you turn over and have to look the boy's mother in the eye and tell her the most painful thing she'll ever hear.

Before we did anything else, Rosie and I prayed. We didn't know much about what had happened, so we prayed for Reggie's health and for his life. We were hoping that it wasn't too serious an accident and that everything would come out all right. But how do you pray intelligently when the matter is urgent and you don't know what to pray for?

When we got to the hospital, they took us to his room. One look told us that our son was no longer with us. Rosie and I just collapsed in each other's arms.

The circumstances of Reggie's death will always remain something of a mystery. The facts of what happened are clear enough. But what Reggie was thinking and why he acted as he did—we'll never know, this side of heaven.

We figured out later that apparently he came by the house soon after Rosie and I had gone to bed that Wednesday night. We had heard someone coming in, and we thought it was Ryan. But it was Reggie, stopping by to get some money. He went back out to meet some friends, and on the way, he was speeding. When he topped a hill, a police car picked him up and put its lights on. For whatever reason, Reggie didn't stop.

The sheriff allowed me to review the dash-cam tape of the pursuit. Reggie got on Interstate 55 north and then exited at Northside Drive, where he stopped. The officer got out and approached Reggie's car. As he came up to the driver's-side window, the tape shows Reggie driving off. We have no way of knowing what the officer said to him.

Reggie sped along Northside until he came over a hill, where a car was turning into his path. According to a neighbor who had heard the siren and came outside to watch the chase, Reggie only had two options: hit the oncoming car, or curve over into the yard of a school where a large tree was standing. Reggie chose the tree.

But before we learned any of those details, in those initial moments of shock Rosie and I slowly tried to absorb the reality of what had just happened. It was now 2:30 in the morning. We didn't know what to do. Thankfully, our friend Neddie Winters had come to the hospital to be with us. We had to decide how to tell Ryan. And

Danita. We had chosen not to wake up Ryan before we left for the hospital. Now we had to drive back home and rouse him from sleep and tell him the horrible news. That was hard.

But it was even harder to know how to tell Danita. She was two hours away in Natchez, southwest of Jackson. Should we call her? We questioned the wisdom of that, since she was in a new community and wouldn't have any close friends to be with. Thankfully, one of the elders from Mendenhall Bible Church, Marcus Turner, along with Neddie Winters, who is also a pastor, stayed with us as we struggled with what we should do. In the end, we decided that we needed to tell Danita in person. Marcus offered to drive with us.

That was the longest drive we've ever taken. All the way, we wondered how Danita was going to handle Reggie's death, because she felt so close to her brother. Finally, we pulled into her driveway. Thank goodness for cell phones! We called her, and she met us at the door. As soon as we walked in, she just said, "Reggie!" Somehow she knew. She'd been tossing and turning all night long. She didn't know how bad it was, but somehow she could just feel that something was wrong. We all just embraced and shed tears together. That was the best decision we ever made, to go there in person and spend that time with her. Both for her sake and ours.

Later that morning after arriving home, we received a phone call from Reggie's girlfriend, Michelle, asking, "Is it true, is it true, is it true...?"

A Time to Heal

The board of Mission Mississippi graciously allowed me to take six weeks off to spend time with my family. That was a very tough six weeks. The accident had occurred on June 23, 2004. Three weeks later we had to deal with Reggie's birthday. I had so many feelings, and so many unanswered questions. What really happened that night? What was going on in Reggie's mind? Why did he run from the police? Why did he stop and then run again? What could I have done differently as a father? Was there something I missed, something I hadn't paid enough attention to? Was there some way in which Reggie's racial heritage played into all of it? Why did my son's life have to end up this way? How was I ever going to recover from this? How would I be able to go on?

Throughout that period of grieving the loss of our son, we received countless phone calls, letters, notes, and cards from people expressing their sorrow and support. However, two calls were particularly significant for me as a father. One was from Leighton Ford, the evangelist, who served with me on the board of World Vision. Like me, Leighton and his wife had had a daughter and two sons. Like me, his older son had died—in his case, following heart surgery in 1981. It was comforting to talk to another father who knew firsthand the pain of losing a son. It also helped me understand what to expect from grief. "Dolphus," he said, "I'm calling to say to you that it will get easier—but it will never go away."

Another call that was especially helpful came from John Huffman, pastor of St. Andrews Presbyterian Church in California, and who was also on the World Vision board. John's twenty-three-year-old daughter, Suzanne, had died of Hodgkin's lymphoma in 1991. Again, it was the voice of a father who understood the loss of a child and could share such a deep, cutting pain.

As we sorted through all the cards and calls and just tried to regain our bearings in the midst of all the grief, we concluded that we needed to do some tangible things to promote our family's healing and bring some meaning to Reggie's death. We decided to do three things, and then later added a fourth that we hadn't anticipated.

First, we chose to create a scholarship fund in Reggie's honor within a foundation that we had created called R.E.A.L. Christian Foundation. Today, the Reggie Weary Memorial Scholarship Fund provides educational scholarships for young African Americans from poor rural communities in Mississippi. That fund currently has about $160,000 in it. My dream is to see it grow to $500,000.

The second decision we made was to find a Christian counselor and process our grief. We knew from experience that I handle my emotions much differently than Rosie handles hers, and Ryan handles his in a different way still. I'm so glad we did that, because one day when we were talking about Reggie's death, I started crying. As soon as Ryan saw that, he started doing his best to comfort me. That's when I realized: Ryan's only sixteen, he needs to be grieving himself rather than feeling like he's got to caretake his mom and dad. So we began meeting with a counselor once a week with all three of us, and then a meeting with Ryan by himself. We did that for two years, gradually moving to every other week, and then once a month. That was so healthy for all of us.

The counseling led to the third conscious decision we made, which was to talk openly as a family about what had happened and how we felt about it. Too many families tiptoe around sensitive topics, or else avoid them altogether. That's poisonous! The grief and the loss and the pain are going to be there regardless of whether anyone is willing to face the situation. At every holiday, every anniversary, every major event in a family's life, the memories are going to come flooding back. Every time you fill out an application, a medical form, an insurance form, or a biographical statement, you come back to the reality that someone in the family is missing. We decided that the healthiest way of handling all of that was just to talk freely and allow ourselves to feel whatever emotions we felt. To do otherwise would border on committing the sin of silence that I talked about earlier, though in a different way.

The fourth choice we made could only have been orchestrated by God. Eight Wednesdays after Reggie was killed, our telephone rang at 11:15 PM, the very same moment when the call had come about Reggie. I picked up the phone, and once again it was a call from a hospital. Only this time, the news was that a little baby boy had been born: Reggie Weary Jr. Rosie and I had a grandson!

Little Reggie's arrival significantly changed our outlook. His presence was like a little miracle. Suddenly, in the midst of all the pain that death had brought into our family, a new life had burst into our world like a shaft of light from heaven, inspiring us with the first real joy and hope we had felt in weeks. And so it didn't take us long to realize that Little Reggie was meant to be the fourth part of our healing process.

Every weekend since he was two weeks old, Rosie and I have been keeping Little Reggie. His father had determined even before his girlfriend's baby was born that he wanted the child to be named Reggie. And it was a good choice, because Little Reggie looks just like his father. So much so that when he sees pictures of Reggie around our house, he says, "That's me!" and we have to say, "No, that's your dad." I know that grandparents always take special pride in their grandchildren, but this little boy has brought nothing short of the joy of the Lord to his adoring grandparents Grandma Rosie and Pops (we taught him to call me Pops).

An Unexpected Gift

In a way, the surprise entrance of Little Reggie into our family was a repeat of the surprise I had experienced when our third child, Ryan, came along. At the time, Danita was thirteen and Reggie was eleven. Rosie and I felt that those were just the right ages for our children to be in light of the traveling I was doing in connection with TMM. Since the kids were no longer infants, we felt comfortable leaving them with family members and close friends sometimes so Rosie could travel with me.

Then Rosie learned that she was pregnant. Rather than telling me straight out, she waited until we exchanged gifts at Christmas. I opened up a box containing a diaper, diaper pins, and other related items. Once I figured out what was going on, I could see that this was going to be a gift that would keep on giving!

And yet the truth was that Rosie and I weren't sure we wanted to go back to the beginning in terms of childrearing. Rosie even went through a period of mild depression over her unplanned pregnancy. That challenged me in my own heart and led me to a time of asking God, "Why?" I began to think about how we could turn this new development into a time of celebration and renewed focus.

I decided to take Rosie to Hawaii for her birthday. We worked out all the details so we were able to get away for a real vacation together. We ended up having a wonderful time, and a lot of that time we spent praying together and reflecting on the new things that God was bringing into our lives. The Lord helped us rethink our whole life process, which began to melt away the depression and anxiety in our hearts. As a result of that time of seeking God, both of us were able to genuinely celebrate our new baby's birth.

But what were we going to name him? With the first two, we had determined to use the "D" from my first name and the "R" from Rosie's first name, regardless of which sequence we used for either child. So we ended up with Danita Ronique and Reginald Demond. With the third child, whom we learned would be a boy, we decided to let Danita and Reggie choose the new names. Reggie decided on Ryan for the first name, and Danita chose Donché for the middle name. So, on July 23, 1987, our family welcomed Ryan Donché Weary into our lives—an unexpected but thoroughly delightful blessing.

We'd already seen how different Danita and Reggie were in terms of gifts, interests, and personalities. Ryan was altogether another new person to discover. Years earlier, we'd bought a piano so Danita and Reggie could take music lessons, but neither of them really stayed with it. Ryan, however, loved to bang on the piano from an early age and began taking lessons when he was six. He also took up the saxophone in junior high school, and to this day spends a lot of time listening to and writing music.

Black and White and Lots of Gray

Just after Ryan graduated from the sixth grade at Genesis One Christian School, our family moved from Mendenhall to Jackson. We were faced with the decision of where Ryan should go to school. Lee Paris, our board chairman at Mission Mississippi, encouraged me to consider Jackson Preparatory School. I could see that a school like Jackson Prep would be ideal for Ryan's interest in music, along with other gifts he possessed. But Jackson Prep was essentially an all-white school. "We don't want him to go to Jackson Prep," I told Lee. "He'd be one of only five blacks in the entire school." Somehow Lee didn't think that would be a problem.

So the next day he asked me about it again. I told him we were still very unsettled about the race issue. Once again, he tried to assure me that all would be okay. So I turned the tables on him. "Lee, let's say that Jackson Prep is everything you want it to be—good teachers, good academics, good everything. But now let's paint the faces of all the people there black. Would you still want your child to go to Jackson Prep?" At that, the lights came on for Lee, and he understood my concerns.

But in the end, Ryan did enroll at Jackson Prep. He willingly accepted the challenge of going to a predominantly white private school, unsure of exactly what the experience would be like. There were about 170 other students in his seventh-grade class, three of whom were black females. Ryan was the only black male in the seventh grade.

As soon as he got home from school the first day, Reggie wanted to know, "How did they treat you? What did they say to you? What did they think about you?" It was all "they, they, they." I realized that talking about the situation in that way would only highlight the racial divide in Ryan's mind. So I took Reggie aside and said, "Listen, we've got to change our language in this house. Ryan's going to that school with the idea of being the best student he can be. For us to teach him the 'they' language, it means that every day he's going to leave here going, 'I wonder how *they* are going to treat me.' He's going to be looking for all those 'they' marks. We want to change our language. We want to ask him, 'How did your day go? Did anything exciting happen for you today? Did you have any challenges today?' Create that kind of conversation, rather than 'they' this and 'they' that."

Reggie accepted my challenge, and it really helped Ryan have a great experience at a new school. He played in the band, which meant he had to travel with the football team to away games. We had to pay attention to that and make sure someone in our family went along to those games, because he was going to other academies, some of which had no black students at all. Without one of us there, he would have been the only black person at those games.

As it turned out, Lee Paris was right that being one of only five black students at Jackson Prep was not going to be a problem for

Ryan. He encountered a few minor struggles, but on the whole, his race was a nonissue. The biggest thing he had to learn to deal with was that every time something racially sensitive happened in the wider culture, the other students expected him to represent the entire black race. They'd ask him, "Why do black people think this way or that way? Why do black people do this or that?" As if *all* black people think and do the same things! Ryan couldn't possibly know how to answer that.

But he'd try! And that began to create a problem. When the white students asked him those questions, he would quickly give them an answer. But then later he would think up a better answer. And so for the rest of the day he would feel badly that he hadn't been able to give the best answer right away. When he would tell me about what happened later, he'd say, "I wasn't smart enough."

I thought, "Wow! That's no good." I knew I had to reorient his thinking. So I told him, "Ryan, none of us is smart enough to represent the whole race. So you don't have to do that. You're just a seventh grader. There's not even an adult who is able to speak for *all* of his race. Let that burden go!"

All in all, Ryan had a great time at Jackson Prep. His spirit was wonderful, and he benefited significantly from the opportunity. Nevertheless, after two years there, he asked Rosie and me if he could switch to the public school in Richland. His reason took me by surprise: he said he felt like he was becoming white and losing contact with his blackness.

I had to really check my spirit when I heard that. All of my work at Mission Mississippi was about looking past racial differences and getting away from the mentality of "we in this race think this way, and 'those people' in that race think that way." But now I had to put on a different hat and see my son as an individual person. He was trying to work out his own sense of identity and how his race entered into that. This was not about what I might have wanted; it was about Ryan and how he was handling that challenge. I had to listen to his heart.

Frankly, I could identify with what he was going through, because I occasionally encounter the exact same thing. One time I was talking politics with a friend who is African American. I mentioned that I'm a registered Democrat. He was shocked, which caught me off guard. So I asked him why he was surprised. "Oh, we thought you'd turned into a Republican," he said. Now I was the one who was surprised! How could anyone ever think that? He said, "Because you're around white people all the time." I just started laughing. That was so crazy! As if all white people are Republicans, and any minority who hangs out with them is a Republican too. (The truth is, I like some things that Republicans stand for, and I question some things that Democrats stand for. But neither party is perfect. So I am very careful to pick and choose among candidates and positions when it comes time to vote. And at Mission Mississippi, I stress that our work is about racial reconciliation within the Christian community, not political affiliations and issues.) The point is, the issue of whether one is "too white" or "not black enough" is something a lot of African Americans have to wrestle with, regardless of age.

In the end, we let Ryan make the decision about where he would go to school. So he picked Richland.

Of course, changing schools meant a new set of challenges. Richland High School was about 70 percent white and 30 percent black. As Ryan began to make friends there, he was surprised to find that he was having a hard time relating to the black students. Every once in a while they would say things to him like, "You sound white!" He began to feel a bit paranoid, as if something was wrong with him. Those comments certainly confirmed his reason for transferring from Jackson Prep. He felt that he needed to regain some of his blackness.

I know that young people in the African-American community really struggle with that tension of, "Am I too white?" or "Am I black enough?" It's a lingering result of racism. Personally, I think that tension may have damaged Ryan a little bit, although he did well at Richland and graduated with flying colors.

After high school, Ryan ended up going to Belhaven University, a Christian liberal arts school in Jackson. He wanted to major in music in order to pursue his lifelong passion. I told him he could do that, but first he had to develop a practical skill that he could bank on in the marketplace. So he majored in business until the end of his junior year, when he changed to marketing and communication. That's when the light came on for Ryan. He found the coursework very exciting, and it dovetails perfectly with his aspirations to have some sort of career related to music.

Recently he was accepted to an internship at WLBT-3, the NBC Television affiliate in Jackson. He's been able to do a little bit of on-air news, and his manager is really pushing him to get involved in every aspect of the station. He's loving it! So it will be interesting to see how it all turns out and where the Lord ultimately leads Ryan as he pursues his career.

A Balancing Act

So now, as you can see, God has given Rosie and me three very different children, plus a grandchild who is unique as well. All four have been unbelievable blessings to us. And all four have gone through things that tested our faith in different ways. Through it all—both in the glad times and in the sad times—God has been faithful. He rarely shows me why things happen the way they do, even though I ask Him why countless times. Most of the time He simply says, "Dolphus, trust Me. I made you. I love you. I've brought you this far. I am with you in this moment. I'm not going anywhere. Rest in Me. Let My purposes do their work."

God's presence has given me a lot of peace, and His guidance has brought a lot of wisdom as well as grace. As with most ministers' families, ours has struggled with giving adequate attention to both our ministry responsibilities and our family's needs. Ministers often reason that since they are doing "the Lord's work," that work should take precedence over their families. Rosie and I never felt right about that sort of thinking. We've tried to be on constant guard against it, starting with our marriage itself.

Early on, as we saw my travel schedule expanding, we determined that Rosie should go with me on ministry trips as often as possible. We wanted to minimize our time apart. Plus, I wanted Rosie to be able to meet and get to know some of the people with whom I was forming relationships. We knew that her traveling with me would cost more money. But we felt it was a small price to pay to make sure we were sharing our lives and our ministry as much as possible. So in the end, we decided that every third time I visited a particular city, Rosie would go with me.

Naturally, my frequent ministry travels significantly affected my availability to the children, particularly the two older ones. Danita had a wonderful spirit in accepting the fact that I had to be on the road a lot. She only asked one big favor of me: promise to call home every day, no matter where I was or how tight my schedule might be (remember, that was in the days of long-distance phone calls, before cell phones were even invented). So a daily check-in became our "father-daughter agreement," a regular habit I followed whenever I traveled. It helped me keep the family aware of what was happening on the road and also to stay on top of what was happening to them back in Mendenhall (this was before we moved to Jackson). It also helped to keep them involved in praying for me and the ministry. That was such an encouragement, because there were so many times when I'd call home and report to the children, "I think God really used me this morning," and they'd reply, "We know! That's exactly what we were praying for."

Still, I know my kids paid a price as a result of the ministry and the travel. Sometimes I look back and feel regret for having missed some key moments as they were growing up. At one point, I was traveling about half of the time. That's when Rosie and I realized we needed to rethink our well-intended decision to try to include her in a lot of the travel. We decided that it was more important for our children to have immediate access to at least one of their parents, especially when they were young. So we made a special effort to limit the time that both of us were away.

One particular scheduling challenge had to do with Reggie's basketball games during his senior year. Because he was a starter on the team, I knew he needed me to be there as much as I could. So I asked him to show me the schedule for the season as soon as he received it. I wrote down all of his games on my calendar, and then I planned my travel schedule around them. I made a conscious decision to decline any speaking engagements that would conflict with one of those games. That season, Reggie's team played about thirty games, and I was able to attend all but three of them, including away games. That was a huge challenge, but I wanted to send a signal to Reggie and everyone else that I was determined to keep family and ministry in balance.

Rosie and I also tried to reflect that balance in how we brought guests into our home. We had a lot of people coming to visit us at Mendenhall—not just individual church leaders and couples, but groups of volunteers and others that sometimes numbered anywhere from twenty to forty people. Their trips to TMM invariably included a visit to the Weary household. There was a lot of value in having our children meet these different visitors. They usually came from different backgrounds, so they were able to expand our kids' horizons. At the same time, we wanted to make sure that "ministry time" didn't eclipse "family time" and that our children weren't overexposed to ministry-related discussions. We wanted them to feel good about the work God had called their parents to do, not be burned out on it.

So whenever we had groups over, we typically would provide some food and share how God was working in Mendenhall. Then we'd invite our guests to ask whatever questions they had. We encouraged our children to participate in those gatherings whenever they wanted to but not to feel obligated to do so. We also kept those visits fairly brief, usually between 7:00 and 9:00 PM, so that the family could have a normal life.

Of course, I talk about a "normal" family life. So what did that mean for an African-American family in Mississippi in the 1980s, '90s, and early 2000s? In most respects, it probably meant that our family looked like most other middle-class families in America. We owned a house. We sent our kids to school. We shopped at the shopping mall. We went to church. In all of those ways and more, we were unremarkable. We were "normal." Normal African Americans, that is. Which meant that at most every moment and in most every situation, our family lived its life against the backdrop of race.

For Danita, that meant having to contend with the low expectations of a ninth-grade counselor at her high school, only to wonder later on at Rhodes whether she really was college material. For Reggie it meant having to contend with teammates on his tennis team who felt he was "invading" what was supposed to be a "white" sport. For Ryan, it meant having to contend with the questions "Am I too white?" or "Am I black enough?" For Rosie and me as parents, it meant having to contend with the lingering effects of decades and centuries of racism, trying our best, in our generation and on behalf of our children, to put a stop, if possible, to a mindset that said, *You're always going to be second-class. It doesn't matter what you do or how hard you work. The system is rigged against you. That's just the way it is, and nothing is ever going to change.*

Praise God, I think we *have* stopped that mind-set in our family! Praise God, I believe things *are* changing for the better in our society for African Americans! Every day I see firsthand ways in which hope is springing to life. I see God doing miracles, both in my life and in the lives of countless people in Simpson County and throughout Mississippi. So I thoroughly reject that ancient mind-set of hopelessness, even though from time to time it raises its ugly head, like a water moccasin that's been killed but can still inflict serious injury as it writhes and twitches.

Later, I'll tell you about some of those hope-filled miracles that God is bringing about. But first, I need to point out that there's a reason why the mind-set of *nothing is ever going to change* lingers for many African Americans. It's because they are not on a level playing field. I say that, fully aware and totally appreciative of the fact that Congress and the courts have actively intervened to ensure justice and equity for all.

But laws do not change a mind-set. Not overnight, anyway. A mind-set is built up over generations, so even when circumstances change and society becomes more accommodating, a person can still suffer from the effects of things that happened long before they were born.

It was the recognition of that lingering mind-set that brought about what we now call affirmative action. Few things have been as controversial—or as misunderstood. Earlier in the book, I mentioned a businessman who asked me, "Dolphus, what do you think about affirmative action?" In the next chapter, I'll tell you.

CHAPTER 7

A Level Playing Field

In this chapter, I want to give some attention to the issue of affirmative action, which has to do with *policy* in regard to correcting racial disparities. And let me just come right out and say that if you are a white male, the odds are high that you won't like affirmative action. Even if you think it might be a good idea in principle, your gut tells you that a vote for affirmative action is a vote against the white male. And in some sense, that may be true. That's one reason why affirmative action is such a controversial topic. It's an attempt to rewrite the rules of the game.

That's why I tease my white male friends by saying, "You white men are an endangered species!" They laugh, but I know a lot of them feel like they really are in danger of extinction. After all, they've seen group after group—from women to African Americans, to Latinos, to other ethnic minorities—gain ground over the years at their expense. Sometimes it only *appears* to be at their expense, and white men have lost nothing. But other times, the gains actually result in white men having to share something that traditionally belonged only to them—notably power and access.

But that gets to the heart of the problem. It's very hard for white males to appreciate just how much, and for how long, things have been stacked in their favor. They may not see it that way, but other groups do. So when one of those other groups tries to level the playing field, white men will perceive it as unfair. But what is unfair are the playing field and the rules that have given an unfair advantage to one group over the others.

Start by Taking the Long View

We experience that dynamic firsthand in Jackson, Mississippi. A lot of white folks who now live out in the suburbs complain about the city. "Things ran a lot better when we lived there," they say. And they tie it to race. "We moved out, the black people moved in, and the city went down." What they don't think about is what happened twenty years earlier. That's when the white business owners moved out to the suburbs. They moved their businesses to the suburbs with them. The blacks who replaced them in Jackson didn't own any businesses to speak of. So without that tax base and the other benefits that a strong economy brings, city services were bound to suffer.

Perhaps the schools have suffered the most. To try to correct that, someone will put together a referendum once in a while to raise some tax money or bond money or whatever. Guess how the folks in the suburbs feel about that? A lot of them are paying for their kids to go to private schools, so they don't want to have to pay more money for the public schools. "That's not our problem. That's something for 'those people' in Jackson to take care of. It's *not fair* to make us pay for 'their' education." And so they vote against improving the schools. Then they turn around and complain about how bad Jackson's schools are!

That kind of shortsightedness will catch up with all of us sooner or later. Without any help, the schools are going to be worse off, and that will only make the city and the whole region worse off. I'm not picking on my city, which I love. I'm just using Jackson as an example because I know its problems firsthand. I could talk about a lot of other cities that I know have similar problems.

When it comes to affirmative action, I always say that you have to look at things over a long history, not just right now. If you only focus on the way things are today, you'll only see the situation in terms of your own self-interest, and you'll fight to keep things as they are. But if you go back and look at what led to the way things are today, you'll begin to see why one group consistently does better than another. It's not because one group is inherently superior to the other. It's because one group has always had more advantages and the other more disadvantages. Those factors significantly affect the outcome of the "game" over time.

When I talk with white folks in Mississippi about race relations, they tend to think about what has happened over the last twenty-five years. When I talk with black folks, they think about what has happened over the last two hundred fifty years! Or at least the last fifty. Fifty years ago, my family could not work for a Fortune 500 company and get stock options. A white family could. So what are the financial results of that? Or think of all the entrepreneurial start-ups that were forming fifty years ago. Whites could get in on the ground floor in buying stock in those companies, and then watch that stock grow over time. Black folks didn't have that option. We do now, but not fifty years ago. So, not surprisingly, there's a lot more wealth in the white community today than in the black community. It's because one group had advantages that the other group didn't have.

Affirmative action is an attempt to give everyone an equal footing to pursue the American dream. But affirmative action has been very controversial because a lot of folks don't understand what it's all about.

Understanding the Need for Affirmative Action

The term *affirmative action* was first used in a specific racial sense by President John F. Kennedy in 1961. However, it was his successor, Lyndon Johnson, who championed affirmative action as a key means of leveling the playing field for blacks in American society. Speaking in 1965 at the commencement of Howard University, a historically black school in Washington, DC, President Johnson gave a stirring speech on why affirmative action was so necessary. He said the Voting Rights Act, which he would soon sign into law, would bring greater freedom to black Americans. Then he cautioned:

> But freedom is not enough. You do not wipe away the scars of centuries by saying: Now you are free to go where you want, and do as you desire, and choose the leaders you please.
>
> You do not take a person who, for years, has been hobbled by chains and liberate him, bring him up to the starting line of a race and then say, "you are free to compete with all the others," and still justly believe that you have been completely fair.
>
> Thus it is not enough just to open the gates of opportunity. All our citizens must have the ability to walk through those gates.

This is the next and the more profound stage of the battle for civil rights. We seek not just freedom but opportunity. We seek not just legal equity but human ability, not just equality as a right and a theory but equality as a fact and equality as a result.

For the task is to give 20 million [African Americans] the same chance as every other American to learn and grow, to work and share in society, to develop their abilities—physical, mental and spiritual, and to pursue their individual happiness.

To this end equal opportunity is essential, but not enough, not enough. Men and women of all races are born with the same range of abilities. But ability is not just the product of birth. Ability is stretched or stunted by the family that you live with, and the neighborhood you live in—by the school you go to and the poverty or the richness of your surroundings. It is the product of a hundred unseen forces playing upon the little infant, the child, and finally the [adult].[1]

Johnson celebrated the fact that the graduates of Howard University would likely go on to enjoy all of the benefits that college-educated, upwardly mobile Americans tend to gain. But he was quick to point out that "for the great majority of [African] Americans—the poor, the unemployed, the uprooted, and the dispossessed—there is a much grimmer story. They still, as we meet here tonight, are another nation. Despite the court orders and the

---

1. President Lyndon Baines Johnson, "To Fulfill These Rights" (commencement address, Howard University, Washington, DC, June 4, 1965), http://www.lbjlib.utexas.edu/johnson/archives.hom/speeches.hom/650604.asp. All related quotations that follow are from this address.

laws, despite the legislative victories and the speeches, for them the walls are rising and the gulf is widening."

Johnson freely admitted that "we are not completely sure why this is. We know the causes are complex and subtle. But we do know the two broad basic reasons." The first, he said, was poverty— "inherited, gateless poverty" that is just as toxic to poor whites as it is to poor blacks. "They lack training and skills. They are shut in, in slums, without decent medical care. Private and public poverty combine to cripple their capacities."

The second reason why generations of black people keep losing ground every day in the battle for true equality, Johnson said, is "much more difficult to explain, more deeply grounded, more desperate in its force. It is the devastating heritage of long years of slavery; and a century of oppression, hatred, and injustice." In other words, a longstanding history of racism.

Racism, Johnson declared, not race, is why black poverty is not the same as white poverty:

> Many of its causes and many of its cures are the same. But there are differences—deep, corrosive, obstinate differences—radiating painful roots into the community, and into the family, and the nature of the individual.
>
> These differences are not racial differences. They are solely and simply the consequence of ancient brutality, past injustice, and present prejudice. They are anguishing to observe. For the [black] they are a constant reminder of oppression. For the white they are a constant reminder of guilt. But they must be faced and they must be dealt with and they must be overcome, if we are ever to reach the time when the only difference between [blacks] and whites is the color of their skin.

To a lot of Americans in 1965, Johnson's words sounded not just liberal, but radical. But they can hardly be viewed as radical today. Regardless of one's opinion of President Johnson and the policies of his administration, there can be no question that he was speaking the truth to America. An ugly, painful truth, and a truth that a lot of Americans, both then and now, didn't and don't like to hear. But the undeniable truth is what it is: ever since Africans were brought to America—and especially because of the way they were brought to America—black people as a race have not been treated with equal dignity, equal opportunity, or equal advantages as other Americans, and particularly white Americans.

Addressing Generational Sin

That is the ugly legacy of slavery, a system energized by the sin of racism. And racism is a generational sin. It not only affects the sinner and the one sinned against; it affects their children, and their grandchildren, and their great-grandchildren, and on and on unless and until someone breaks the cycle by repenting of the sin and taking action to replace sin with God's grace.

That's what all of us have to remember. All of us are dealing with things that took place long before any of us showed up. It's why I say that we can't just focus on the way things are today. We have to go back and look at what led to the way things are today. We can't do anything about what happened in the past, but we certainly can do something now to mitigate if not eliminate the terrible effects of what happened in the past.

None of us were there. None of us participated in the system of slavery. Yet in a real sense, all of us were there, because our forefathers were there, and to this day their legacy remains with us. They are not here anymore, so it's up to us to clean up the mess they left us. It's exactly as Moses warned: "The LORD is slow to anger and abundant in lovingkindness, forgiving iniquity and transgression; but He will by no means clear the guilty, visiting the iniquity of the fathers on the children to the third and the fourth generations" (Numbers 14:18 NASB).

These are hard things to talk about. And my point is not to play the blame game. We're all caught up in a broken, sinful world. All I'm trying to do here is to show why many black Americans want the rules of the game to be rewritten. Because the game has been unfair to black folks for so long, as Lyndon Johnson said, even court orders and laws and legislative victories and speeches haven't put everyone on an equal footing. The starting line for too many blacks is way behind the rest of the pack. So if we leave things as they are, how can they ever catch up?

Affirmative action is just a strategy of intentionally helping black Americans catch up to everyone else. In its simplest form, it's a policy that says, if two candidates apply for the same position and they are equally qualified to do the job, the nod goes to the minority. It's really no different than what happens at a lot of colleges and universities in terms of how they break a tie when it comes to admissions. If the choice is between you and someone else who is equally qualified, and one of your parents graduated from the school and the other person's did not, they admit you over that other person. That policy is an intentional way of attracting family members of alumni.

Is Affirmative Action Fair or Unfair?

"But that's unfair," someone will say. How so? Once two individuals are equally qualified, qualifications are no longer the deciding factor. Something else must be considered other than qualifications.

A school may choose to give the nod to children of alumni, but they could just as easily decide on another basis—say, the likelihood of one set of parents making a large donation to the school. Or a prospective student's intention of majoring in electrical engineering rather than marketing. Or the fact that one of the applicants is from Asia and will help to broaden the school's cultural diversity. Why, if it wanted to, the school could give preference to an applicant with red hair! It's totally the school's prerogative.

"No, but it's still unfair. It discriminates against people whose parents didn't graduate from the school." But that's not discrimination, because whether your parents graduated from the school is not a qualification for admittance. It's a consideration to be made *after* all the other qualifications have been met.

In its purest form, affirmative action is a policy that considers race after all the other qualifications have been met.

But that will still feel unfair to many white people. If, for example, they lose out in a hiring situation because of affirmative action, they will likely argue that "the only reason the other person got the job is because they were black." To which I would argue, no, that person got the job because they were *qualified*. The employer had two equally qualified candidates—you and the black person. They went with the black person because they are trying to be intentional about helping black Americans catch up to everyone else.

You see, we wouldn't be having this discussion if things had been truly equal and "fair" all the way along. But the truth is they have not. The doors have always been open to white males. But for a long time, a black person couldn't get hired, period. No matter how qualified they might have been. Was that fair? Then it became that they couldn't get hired unless they were many times more qualified than any white applicant. Was that fair? Then it became that if a black person and a white person were equally qualified, the nod just somehow always went to the white person. Was that fair?

But more recently, we've got a few employers who have decided they really want to see black folks have a shot at the American dream. So if they have two candidates who are *equally qualified*, one black and one white, they are free to hire whichever one they please. If they choose to hire the black person, how is that unfair? Certainly, it will be a disappointment to the white candidate. But if the black person is qualified, hiring him or her cannot be called unfair.

What if they picked the white person? Would that be unfair? No, but it would be unfair if they *always* hired a white person and never a black person. And that's what happened for a long, long time, and in some places still happens to this day. Affirmative action recognizes that disparity. It's an attempt to change a system that traditionally has been unfair to blacks and others. But for some white people, a decision is only "unfair" if the white person doesn't get picked.

One way that opponents of affirmative action seek to subvert it is to become very legalistic and technical about the meaning of "equally qualified." For instance, two job applicants take a test. One scores 97 out of 100, the other scores 95. The person who wants to split hairs will argue that the one who scored 97 is the *most* qualified. But the truth is, they are *both* qualified. Especially if all the other applicants who took the test scored in the 80s and 70s. And also if the test score is just one of many qualifications used to make the hire. Nevertheless, some people will go to great lengths to keep a black person from getting ahead.

The Importance of Policy

I say "some people," but by no means everyone. I believe a majority of Americans today agree that blacks have traditionally been at a decided disadvantage socially and economically, and they'd like to see that change. But they wonder: why do we need a *policy* to make that happen? The answer is because we human beings have short memories. We're great at talking about all of our good intentions. But as soon as the tyranny of the urgent comes along, we get distracted, and our good intentions fade out.

That's why, at Mission Mississippi, we put it in writing as a policy that we would always stay focused on race. That's our issue: racial reconciliation. People often ask us to get involved in other causes, some of which are related to race. What about gender? Economics? Community development? Politics? Those kinds of issues are certainly important. But we feel the best way we can contribute to them is to foster racial reconciliation based on the gospel. If we can get white Christians and black Christians to form relationships and experience honest communication based on mutual trust, respect, and friendship, that will significantly benefit all the other conversations that need to take place. By having a written policy statement that nails down racial reconciliation as Mission Mississippi's primary focus, we guard against losing sight of our core concern.

A similar approach was taken by the board of an international ministry on which I serve. The ministry decided to make multi-ethnicity a priority. We saw that our work around the world was increasingly attracting numerous internationals onto our staff and into leadership positions, and we wanted the ministry to respond to that diversity in everything we were doing and how we operated. So we established a policy to spell out what that would look like.

Shortly after formulating that policy, we did a search for a new president. The candidate we fell in love with was an outstanding leader with very impressive credentials, experience, and qualifications. As we were going through the interview process, I thought about our policy on multiethnicity. So I began asking the candidate some questions about his experience with a multiethnic organization. He was honest about the fact that he didn't have much experience in that. "You have no experience crossing out of your white box," I stated out loud, to make sure all the other board members understood the situation—and also that he understood our concern in light of our policy. I wasn't trying to criticize him. I just thought it was vitally important for everyone to know that we would be hiring a president who had a lot to learn about multiethnicity and racial reconciliation. It wouldn't necessarily take him long to get up to speed on those issues. And in the end we hired him knowing that he had a fairly steep learning curve ahead of him in this regard. But I was sure thankful for that policy statement, because without it, it wouldn't take long for the tyranny of the urgent to crowd out any attention a new president might give to multiethnicity.

Policy is a discipline that ensures that we follow through on our good intentions. It's an objective reminder of what we said we want to do and be. And intentionality is the key when it comes to affirmative action. If you really want to rewrite the rules on race and ethnicity, you have to be deliberate in how you go about doing that. It can't just be tokenism.

I was on the board of Belhaven University, a Christian liberal arts school in Jackson. They had a vision for becoming a multiracial campus, with students from many racial and ethnic backgrounds. As they wrestled with the possibilities and the challenges of doing that, they asked for my thoughts. I said, "Guys, if you decide to be a multiracial campus, you have to make it multiracial throughout the school." They pointed out that minorities already comprised 20 percent of their student body. I said, "That's a good start. But how many people of different races do you have on your faculty? On your board? On your coaching staff? On your administrative staff? How will you handle the chapel program and the chapel speakers, if you're really going to be a multiracial school? It's easy if you have just one predominant race on campus. But when you start talking about multiple races and ethnic groups, you've got to take *all* those groups into account all throughout the organization."

You see, affirmative action is ultimately about sharing power. It's not about the white people in a situation staying in power and then using that power to be kind to the other groups. No, it's about putting all the groups on an equal footing, and all of them having a seat at the table. You can never have that if one group is always in charge.

Easier Said Than Done

Now let's be honest: there is no end of the challenges in trying to change a situation where one group has always been in charge to a situation where power is shared by different groups. It's hard on *everybody*. It's hard on the group that has always been in charge, because it feels like they are losing control, at least early on. That can feel scary. But it's also hard on the groups that suddenly find themselves with new authority and responsibility. The big question that always looms over them is, can they handle it?

I remember when I was on the development committee of a board one time, and they were beginning to discuss how to make their board more diverse in terms of ethnicity and gender. So I was at a meeting one day, and the other committee members, who were all white, started talking about finding "qualified" minorities and "qualified" women to serve on the board. I listened for a while. Finally, I said, "Hold on, guys. We need to change our language. Let's just talk about finding board members. Let's talk about finding some women for the board, and let's talk about finding some minorities for the board. Period! Let's not use the term 'qualified' for these people. To be on this board, 'qualified' is always a given. Otherwise, using that term is a negative against minorities and women."

Later, I said the same thing to the board as a whole: "We're never again going to look for any 'qualified' minorities. We're never again going to look for any 'qualified' women. We're just going to look for board members. Because when you talk about white men, you don't talk about 'qualified' white men. You just find white men who meet the qualifications to be on the board. Period!"

I was pretty forceful in how I said that. So when I was finished, the other board members just sat there and looked at me for a moment. They finally said, somewhat cautiously, "Okaaay!" Then we all started laughing. One of them shook his head and spoke for the rest of them, "We don't know what to do with you, Dolphus!" But afterward, a number of them came up to me and said, "Man, you're right!"

Changing the rules of the game is hard on the people who have always been in charge. But it may be even harder on the people who are finally getting a seat at the table. To be the first minority to break through a traditional barrier is a tremendous challenge. The expectations are always sky high. In fact, it's as if you have to be twice as good as anyone else would have been in the situation, because everyone is kind of waiting for you to fail.

When Jackie Robinson became the first African-American player in Major League Baseball in 1947, he endured blatant bigotry his entire first season. Some of his teammates refused to sit on the bench with him. The St. Louis Cardinals threatened to strike if they had to play against him. The manager of the Philadelphia Phillies shouted the N-word at him from the dugout and told him to go back to picking cotton. And he was the constant target of physically aggressive play by opposing teams. Nevertheless, Robinson was awarded Major League Baseball's first National League Rookie of the Year Award after he finished that initial season with 12 home runs, a .297 batting average, 125 runs scored, and 29 steals (the most in the league).

That's a storybook ending, and it makes every African American proud. But what would have happened if Jackie Robinson had been just another pretty good baseball player, instead of a superstar? Would people have said, "See, that shows that a black man shouldn't be playing this game"? All I know is, no one would have considered race when evaluating the performance of a white player.

Living Up (or Down) to Expectations

When Danita first got to Rhodes College, she would call home in tears. "Daddy, this is so hard! These subjects are so hard! All my friends are out having fun. They don't have to study. It's all so easy for them. But I'm working so hard." She was struggling to learn the material, and she was beginning to doubt whether she was intelligent enough to be at Rhodes.

I told her, "Danita, it has nothing to do with your ability or intelligence. It has an awful lot to do with your background and what you were exposed to. You've got to understand that most of those other students were being prepared to come to a college like Rhodes from their earliest days. They were brought up in all the right schools. They were put in special programs. They've been able to read more books than you've even thought about. They've been able to do things you never dreamed of, like spending a year in Italy or whatever. You went to little old Mendenhall High School. That school barely had the means of getting you through algebra. They thought you'd be fine if you just graduated and went to vocational school. They weren't thinking you'd end up at Rhodes College and start taking courses to be a doctor.

"So you see, college is going to be a lot harder for you, because you're starting from a different place. No one except your mama and me ever thought you'd go this far. But for most of your friends there, the preparation and exposure and expectations about succeeding have always been in their minds. They grew up in a system that prepared them to go to a college like Rhodes. You've not been in a system that prepared you to go to Rhodes."

I just ached for my daughter, because I knew she was discovering firsthand some of the disadvantages that blacks have inherited. There was no question that she was fully qualified to get into Rhodes. They even gave her an academic scholarship because of her record of achievement. That still didn't change the fact that Danita was starting way behind the rest of the pack and having to catch up. Eventually, she did catch up, but not without wondering many times, "Do I really have what it takes?" I know that many a young person worries whether they have what it takes when they get to college. But for an African American, there's always the lingering issue of race: "Am I here because I deserve to be here, or is it because they had to let some black kids in, and I was the one who got selected?"

That kind of second-guessing shows just how damaging it can be to grow up with diminished expectations about what a person can amount to. If your society tells you that you can't go very far and if your community doesn't invest in you to go very far and if your parents themselves haven't gone very far and if they don't believe in you or encourage you to go very far, guess what? You're not going to go very far.

That's the way it's been in rural Mississippi for generations. Rural blacks traditionally never went to college. Many of them never even graduated from high school. The prevailing mind-set was: *It doesn't matter what you do about schooling, you won't be able to find a job anyway. And even if you do find one, it won't pay enough to live on. You're always going to be the last to get hired and the first to get fired. You're going to get passed over for promotions. So why even try?*

That's the culture I returned to when I came back to Mendenhall in the summer of 1968, before my senior year of college. I couldn't find a job. Fortunately, I had John Perkins in my life, and he started talking to me about creating my own job. You see, the only jobs available to me as a rising senior in college were the same old menial jobs that had been available when I was a senior in high school.

John pointed out, "What kind of an impact are you going to have on the young people around here if you're out there in the cotton fields working alongside them? That's going to send the message that education doesn't matter. That they can go all the way through college, like Dolphus has, but they're still going to end up right back in the cotton fields." Thanks to John, I found a job that was worthy of my true skills.

Who is setting the expectations for the young people in our communities? That's the question on which the entire future of a generation hangs. Will they have someone coming alongside them saying, "You can do it! You can make something of yourself! You have what it takes! You need to start preparing yourself and getting ready to take advantage of your opportunity when it comes." And of course, along with the encouragement and hope, those young people have to have real options that open the door to a brighter future.

But if they don't have that voice somewhere in their life—and

I'm afraid too many of them today don't—they for sure will have voices telling them that it doesn't matter if they study or work hard, nothing is ever going to change, they're just stuck in a bad situation, and the future is hopeless. When those kinds of voices carry the day, young people are suckers for immediate gratification: gangs, drugs, sex.

Sometimes I talk with young African-American boys who are playing around with dope. They like the instant high it gives them. They also like the quick, easy money they get from selling it. Never mind that there are only two outcomes to all of that: prison or death. So I'll ask them, "Don't you know that eventually this is going to catch up with you?" They'll answer, "Sure, we know that. We know we're probably going to prison. We know we might get killed. But in the meantime, we're going to live big." Their horizon is very narrow, because they assume they're never going to have a job. They may end up in prison or worse, but they assume that's going to happen anyway, *with or without the dope!* So why not live it up? Society gets all exercised about the drugs, but the real problem is that no one is offering them any hope.

Changing a Mind-Set

Ironically, the welfare system itself sometimes encourages people to take that short, limited view and look for the quick fix. A few years ago, a young woman who had moved away from Mendenhall, gotten married, had children, and then divorced came back home. Her kids were ages two, four, and six. She desperately needed a job. So we trained her to do some work in the office at TMM and hired her part-time. As soon as she started receiving a paycheck, the government began cutting back on her welfare benefits. She really needed the Medicaid part of those benefits because her second child was severely asthmatic. When she realized the aid was going to go away, she wanted to quit.

I talked to her about her situation. She was saying, "Oh, I can just live at home. I can get more money and free stuff by staying at home with my kids than by coming in here to work. It's just going to hurt me if I come to work."

I said, "Listen, it's important to work *for you*, but it's more important that you work *for your children*. Your children need to see you bringing home a paycheck. Your children need to see you doing something that's benefiting your family now as well as in the future, and not just sitting around waiting for someone to take care of you. By coming to work every day at the ministry, you're going to teach your children a new way of doing life."

To my delight, she accepted the challenge. She got additional training and became a good administrative assistant. Then she got a better job with even better pay, and she's been working there for the past fifteen years. A couple of years ago in December, one of her daughters graduated from college. The next May, she and her other daughter both graduated from college. Now all three of them are working on their master's degrees. How fantastic is that! But it took some encouragement on my part, some determination on her part, and some intentionality on everyone's part to break the cycle of poverty.

That's almost always what it takes: someone to intervene and change a person's mind-set, to raise their expectations. And then that person has to be willing to step out and do something different, because the system has a way of keeping them in the cycle big-time!

Affirmative action can be a powerful tool in breaking that cycle. I don't pretend to have the wisdom of Solomon for answering all of the complicated questions affirmative action raises. But this I know: equality is not just about today; it's about what happened yesterday that has led to today. Two people can stand at the door of opportunity and look like they both have the same shot at success. But if you discover that one has had every benefit in the book while the other has been denied those benefits time and again, that's not a level playing field. Someone has an unfair advantage. If an entire system operates that way and keeps allowing the favored ones to win the game, it won't take long for the people who keep losing to quit the game.

CHAPTER 8

Building Bridges of Reconciliation

Throughout this book I've used the term *racial reconciliation*. What exactly does that mean?

In 1991, a black motorist in Los Angeles named Rodney King was severely beaten by police officers following a high-speed chase. A bystander videotaped the incident, and when the footage aired on national television, the black community erupted with outrage against the Los Angeles Police Department. With racial tension at a fever pitch, the trial was moved from Los Angeles County to nearby Ventura County. When the officers were acquitted, riots broke out, resulting in more than fifty deaths and thousands of injuries, thousands of fires, and nearly $1 billion in financial losses.

One of the most prominent incidents that occurred during the riots took place in South Central Los Angeles only three hours after the verdict was handed down. Outnumbered police had been ordered to retreat from a rapidly growing band of rioters. When a white truck driver named Reginald Oliver Denny stopped at a traffic light, the mob hauled him from his vehicle and beat him senseless. Someone even threw a cinder block on his head as he lay in the street. A helicopter hovering overhead captured the entire incident live. Almost instantly, the entire nation was plunged into an ugly, emotional debate over the relationship between blacks and whites.

Minutes after the Denny beating, an immigrant from Guatemala named Fidel Lopez suffered a similar fate. One rioter used a car stereo to smash open his forehead, while another tried to cut off his ear. When Lopez finally passed out, bystanders sprayed black paint on his chest and genitals. That violence was also caught on videotape, adding fuel to the fire.

On the third day of the riots, Rodney King—the man who had run from the police and was beaten—appeared in front of television news cameras to appeal for calm. He seemed visibly stunned by all the turmoil his story was creating. At a loss for words, all he could manage was a question: "Can we all get along? Can we get along? Can we stop making it . . . making it horrible for the older people and the kids? . . . Please, we can get along here. We all can get along. I mean, we're all stuck here for a while. Let's try to work it out. Let's try to beat it. Let's try to beat it. Let's try to work it out."[1]

Is that what racial reconciliation means—that we all just learn to "get along"? Does it mean just doing the best we can to avoid trouble, since "we're all stuck here for a while"? Will good intentions alone prevent us from "making it horrible" for one another? Or does reconciliation involve something more, something deeper than just trying to "work it out"?

When I became the leader of Mission Mississippi, I needed an-

---

1. Rodney King, May 1, 1992, quoted in Ralph Keyes, *The Quote Verifier: Who Said What, Where, and When* (New York: St. Martin's Press, 2006), vii.

swers for questions like that. I found them where I always find ultimate truth and wisdom—in the Bible. So in this chapter, I want to look at a passage in the New Testament that speaks directly to the issue of reconciliation. It describes how God has built a bridge between Himself and humanity, and how that bridge allows human beings to build bridges between one another, even across racial divides.

How in the World Did They Build It?

According to the National Bridge Inventory from the Federal Highway Administration of the US Department of Transportation, there are nearly six hundred thousand bridges in the United States of America.[2] They vary widely in terms of size, length, design, and capacity. But every one of them has the same purpose—to connect two pieces of land where a gap exists.

Every now and then I drive from Jackson, Mississippi, to New Orleans, and just before I get to The Big Easy, as that city is nicknamed, I have to cross a bridge over Lake Pontchartrain. Lake Pontchartrain is the second-largest saltwater lake in the country, which means that the causeway is one of the longest bridges in the world, spanning over twenty-three miles of water. Oftentimes as I cross that enormous span, I find myself asking, how in the world did they build this?

I wonder the same thing when I occasionally have the privilege of traveling to San Francisco and driving across the Golden Gate Bridge, which connects San Francisco with Marin County. That towering suspension bridge is even more impressive than the Lake Pontchartrain Causeway, because it was built over a channel that

---

2. Hamid Ghasemi, "Bridging the Data Gaps," *Public Roads* 70, no. 6 (May/June 2007), http://www.fhwa.dot.gov/publications/publicroads/07may/02.cfm.

is five-hundred feet deep, is roiled by tides and currents between San Francisco Bay and the Pacific Ocean, is framed by hills that funnel fierce winds into the "gate" between them, and is blanketed by blinding fog on many days of the year. Given all of those challenges, one wonders, how in the world did they build it?

I want you to keep those images of bridge building in mind as you read the following passage from 2 Corinthians 5:14–21:

> For Christ's love compels us, because we are convinced that one died for all, and therefore all died. And he died for all, that those who live should no longer live for themselves but for him who died for them and was raised again.
>
> So from now on we regard no one from a worldly point of view. Though we once regarded Christ in this way, we do so no longer. Therefore, if anyone is in Christ, he is a new creation; the old has gone, the new has come! All this is from God, who reconciled us to himself through Christ and gave us the ministry of reconciliation: that God was reconciling the world to himself in Christ, not counting men's sins against them. And he has committed to us the message of reconciliation. We are therefore Christ's ambassadors, as though God were making his appeal through us. We implore you on Christ's behalf: Be reconciled to God. God made him who had no sin to be sin for us, so that in him we might become the righteousness of God.

Just as the physical terrain of the earth has all kinds of gaps and divides that separate one place from one another, so we find that there are also many gaps and divides that separate people from one another. We find that we are divided internationally. We find divisions regionally and locally. We find divisions between cities and suburbs, between large cities and small towns, between urban areas and rural areas. We find divisions between religious groups, political groups, and public interest groups. We see the sexes divided by the age-old puzzle of male versus female. We find divisions between old and young, between rich and poor, between the haves and the have-nots. Even among Christians, we find divisions between denominations and the various Christian traditions.

And of course, as I have pointed out already in this book, humanity is severely divided racially and ethnically. Racial strife is not just an American problem: it is a worldwide problem. You can find it among the Balkan countries of Eastern Europe. Among the former Soviet countries of Central Asia. In Iraq and throughout the Middle East. Between the Israelis and the Palestinians. Between Israel and the Arab states. In India and Pakistan. In China. In Indonesia. In the jungles of South America. In the simmering tribal rivalries that persist throughout Africa. It seems that wherever groups identify themselves as belonging to one race or ethnic group, they almost automatically become the enemies of other groups.

Why Can't We All Just Be "Americans"?

One approach to "solving" this problem has been to adopt a "melting pot" mind-set. In other words, let's act as if race and ethnicity don't matter. That thinking is especially common in the United States, where the question is often posed: why do we need racial designations at all? Groups describe themselves as African Americans, Hispanic or Latino Americans, Asian Americans, and so on. Why can't we all just be "Americans"?

At first glance, putting things that way sounds reasonable. It seems to promote the commonality and unity of all Americans as equal citizens under the Constitution, with liberty and justice for all. I'm all for that. But where it breaks down is when we start asking, what does a true "American" look like? The answer is that a lot of true "Americans" look a lot different from us!

Think back to what happened at the beginning of World War II. Within weeks after the Japanese attacked Pearl Harbor, President Franklin Roosevelt signed an executive order by which anyone in the United States with as little as one-sixteenth Japanese heritage could be placed in an internment camp. Thousands of Japanese had immigrated to America during the first half of the twentieth century. Ninety percent of them had settled in California, where they used their knowledge of agriculture to prosper. But as with most immigrants when they first arrive, the Japanese were deeply mistrusted and subjected to considerable racial prejudice. When the order came to resettle them in what were called War Relocation Camps, the predominantly white majority on the West Coast hailed the decision. Many publicly voiced their hope that the camps would be the end of the Japanese farmers. No one seemed bothered by the fact that the vast majority of those interned were full-fledged, native-born United States citizens—loyal and patriotic citizens, to boot.

If you are a white person, I hope, in light of painful memories like this in our country's history, that you can appreciate the perspective of non–white Americans, who are liable to feel a bit cynical when someone asks, "Why can't we all just be Americans?" If the person asking that is white, the question comes across as: why can't we all be *white*? In other words, why can't other groups think/act/believe/see the world as white people do? I doubt that most white people who ask that even realize how other groups are perceiving them. But that is what the other groups are hearing.

Consider the infamous O. J. Simpson verdict as an example.

In 1995, football and movie star O. J. Simpson, a black man, was acquitted of murdering his wife, Nicole Brown Simpson, a white woman, and her friend, Ron Goldman, also white. Tens of millions of people watched the announcement of the jury's verdict live on television. As soon as it came, a huge divide became apparent in how blacks and whites saw the trial. Many blacks cheered wildly, while whites sat stunned—not just at the jury's acquittal of a man they felt certain had committed the grisly murders, but at the overwhelmingly positive reaction of the black community to the outcome. (I suppose they were as shocked by the joy of the black people as I had been shocked by the joy of the white students at my college who cheered when Martin Luther King Jr. was assassinated.)

Why did blacks hail the not-guilty verdict, even though polls later showed that a majority of them doubted O. J.'s innocence? I won't presume to speak for all blacks, of course. But consider how you would feel if throughout your life you've watched members of your race stand trial in a system dominated by another group's culture, and time and again members of your race are found guilty by that system—oftentimes despite a lack of evidence, or even despite evidence of innocence—and they are sent to prison. Imagine if your group has a long history of mistrust against the police—a factor that played significantly into how evidence and testimony were collected and interpreted in the O. J. trial. Imagine if throughout your life you've watched members of another group, when they are accused of crimes, appear to beat the system by hiring high-priced lawyers to defend themselves.

Now you have a member of your own group who has been overwhelmingly successful in a society dominated by another group. He is accused of serious crimes, but he is able to afford those high-priced lawyers. They make the case that police mistakes and that prejudice have led to the indictment of an innocent man. For once, will all of that be enough to convince a jury to acquit—again, in a system dominated by the other group's culture? This time it was, and blacks nationwide celebrated the verdict as a victory at last for a black man.

I'm not arguing whether all of those perceptions were valid. I'm just pointing out how different the perceptions of the murder case and verdict were between many blacks and many whites—dramatic differences, despite the fact that both groups overwhelmingly believed O. J. was guilty. If nothing else, those differences highlighted just how enormous the divide can be between two races: as wide as the span across Lake Pontchartrain and as deep as the murky, shark-infested, five-hundred-foot-deep chasm between San Francisco and Marin County.

What Does "American" Look Like?

So can we all just be Americans? I believe we can, but it means we have to accept that different groups bring different perceptions and perspectives to almost every issue. That won't sit well with those who, when they say they want to do away with racial distinctions, mean doing away with everyone else's racial distinctions, *but not their own.* That won't work, because it's impossible to do away with racial distinctions. I can no more "do away" with my blackness than a white person can "do away" with his or her whiteness.

Race is both physical and cultural. Although, by definition, race relates to physical characteristics, it cannot be separated from culture. The physical side is easy to see. But the cultural side is more subtle. Culture extends to language, words, expressions, and ways of communicating, both verbal and nonverbal. It has to do with customs, traditions, values, rituals, and symbols. It involves stories, memories, histories, genealogies, and myths. It may include religious dimensions: how one perceives God or the gods, how one relates to nature, how one thinks about this life and the afterlife. Culture even affects people's psychology: how one thinks about oneself in relation to one's people, how one sees one's place in the world. And also how one regards one's group in relation to other groups in the world. Things like these are deeply ingrained in a human being's very soul. To think that we can just "do away" with them is utterly unrealistic and foolish.

Nor is it preferable to "do away" with racial distinctions. The fact is, there is both beauty and strength in the diversity of human races and cultures. Clearly, Jesus implied the reality of that observation by sending His followers to "make disciples of *all* nations" (Matt. 28:19, emphasis added). The word "nations" is a translation of the Greek word from which we get the adjective *ethnic* and the noun *ethnicity*. There's a lot we could say about living out our commission as Christ's followers, but there's no escaping the fact that Jesus intends people from *every* human grouping—no matter how humans classify themselves by ethnicity, race, tribe, or clan—to become part of His church. That's been going on for two thousand years, before any of us showed up. It continues around the world today in an unprecedented way. Jesus is *for* "all nations."

Christ's ultimate aim is to bring together people from "every nation, tribe, people and language" (Rev. 7:9) and make them *one* (see John 17:20–23). There is no indication that racial or cultural distinctions are supposed to be eliminated. Instead, what will be eliminated are sins like prejudice, bigotry, injustice, and arrogance that use racial or cultural distinctions to divide groups from one another.

We are a long way from fully realizing Christ's vision of unity.

Rather than learning to celebrate our differences and genuinely enjoy and benefit from them, we still harbor race-related sin in our hearts, which all too often stirs up mistrust and fear in us when we are dealing with members of other groups. Without Christ's love ruling our hearts, we end up sinning against others and perpetuate the divisions.

The Greatest Bridge Ever Built

Which brings us back to the analogy of the bridge. As I said earlier, when I drive across a magnificent bridge, I'm always amazed. How in the world did they build this thing? I know that civil engineers and other experts understand the kind of skill and materials that are required to span a gap that may be many miles wide. But how does one span the countless gulfs that separate human groups from each other? A physical bridge may be highly complex, but with the right design, it can be built and remain standing. But bridges across racial divides seem to defy construction. That's because they are ultimately spiritual in nature. Bridging them is not merely difficult; it borders on the impossible, at least for sinful human beings.

That's why, as amazing as bridges like the Lake Pontchartrain Causeway and the Golden Gate Bridge may be, none of them compares to the greatest bridge that has ever been built in all the history of the world. That's the bridge that God built to span the chasm that exists between Him and sinful human beings. That gulf exists because of our sin—not only our race-related sins, but all the other sins that result from our sinful, fallen condition as the human race. "All have sinned," Romans 3:23 tells us, "and fall short of the glory of God."

The words "fall short" paint a very bleak picture. Imagine every human being standing on one side of the Grand Canyon and God standing on the other side. That puts a chasm anywhere between four and eighteen miles wide between us. Will any human, on his or her own, be able to jump that span? The current record for a long jump is held by Mike Powell of the United States. In 1991 at the World Track and Field Championships in Tokyo, he managed to leap 29 feet, 4.5 inches. For women, Galina Chistyakova of the Soviet Union recorded a jump of 24 feet, 8.25 inches at Leningrad in 1988.

The point is that while some people might be able to jump farther out over the Grand Canyon than others, not a single one of us is going to be able to make it safely to the other side. The canyon is simply too wide. The same is true concerning the spiritual canyon that lies between us and God. Some of us might be able to jump farther than others, spiritually speaking. For example, we can think of great moral leaders like Mother Teresa or Billy Graham or Martin Luther King Jr. or Mahatma Ghandi. And most of us can think of people we admire for their integrity, strength of character, or kind and loving manner. But the spiritual gulf between us and God is like the Grand Canyon. It is so vast and wide that none of us—not even the best among us—is able on our own to make it safely to the other side. We all "fall short."

But what humans cannot do, God is able to do, and has done. He has built a bridge across that gulf. When Jesus hung on the cross at Calvary, He became the Bridge whereby any person can come across safely to the other side. He accomplished that incredible result for every single human being—no matter how "good" they may seem (from a human perspective) or how "bad" they may appear (again, from the human perspective). The Bible says, "While we were still sinners, Christ died for us" (Rom. 5:8).

So it doesn't matter what you've done on this side of the gulf, nor does it matter who you are on this side of the gulf. Jesus made it possible for every one of us to have access to a holy God. That's why I say without reservation that God is the greatest Bridge Builder the world has ever known, and Christ is the greatest Bridge the world has ever seen.

That's good news for anyone, but it's especially good news for the person who feels marginalized by racism. One of the worst effects of growing up in a racially prejudiced society is that you feel inferior for the rest of your life. You live with shame, often reinforced by a derogatory label (think of the N-word). So when you hear that you are separated from God by your own sinfulness, it feels like one more rejection, one more message that you are no good, and you don't count, and nothing is ever going to change that.

The Bridge That Is Open to All

The good news of the Bridge Builder is that *anybody* can cross over the Bridge and have a relationship with Him. A man whose people were both the victims of a racist government and the perpetrators of racial prejudice came to Jesus, and He told the man that when it comes to crossing over the Bridge in order to receive God's love, "whosoever" will may come (John 3:16 KJV). *Whosoever,* regardless of what "labels" they might wear. Later, as Jesus breathed out His life on the cross, He cried, "It is finished" (John 19:30). He meant that any human being could now have access to the kingdom of God.

In response to that good news, I can't help but shout out, "Hallelujah! Praise His name!" It is so good to know that *anybody* can cross the Bridge!

Anybody can cross. And guess what? God doesn't have to check it out with you or me first. Isn't that something! You and I don't get to decide who crosses the Bridge. That's good, because if God did ask us, chances are good that there are a whole lot of people whom we think should *not* be allowed across the Bridge.

Isn't that true? I suspect you can think of someone—or maybe a whole group of people somewhere in the world—whom you believe don't deserve to go across the Bridge. I know I can. Thankfully, God doesn't ask me, and He doesn't ask you. Better yet, thank God He doesn't ask anyone whether they feel you and I deserve to cross the Bridge. Rather, God welcomes *anybody* who comes to Him in true repentance and faith. *All* are invited to cross the Bridge of God's salvation.

That is really cause to be glad! That is truly good news! The gospel of Jesus Christ says that those who are rich, those who are not so rich, those who are actually poor, and even those who are considered the scum of the earth are all invited to cross the Bridge. It doesn't matter if *I* think someone doesn't fit into *my* agenda, *my* standards, or *my* race. God's Bridge is *His* Bridge. He owns it, and He doesn't have to ask for anyone's permission or approval on who is allowed to cross that Bridge.

So have you crossed the Bridge and entered into a relationship with God? If not, nothing else in this chapter is going to make sense. Because in order to build bridges between ourselves and other people, we first must have a bridge established between ourselves and the God who loves us. We can't express His love until first we have entered into His love. That's why the Bridge of God's salvation is the most important bridge we will ever be invited to cross. It is vital that we do so. *Everything* depends on it!

A New Identity

Once we have crossed that Bridge and have a genuine relationship with God because Christ now is living inside of us, there's a second bridge to consider. It's a bridge that God calls us as His people to build and to cross over. It's a bridge between ourselves and other people.

Recall the Scripture passage we looked at earlier in 2 Corinthians 5. It said that "if anyone is in Christ, he is a new creation; the old has gone, the new has come! All this is from God, who reconciled us to himself through Christ" (vv. 17–18). So God has built a Bridge between us and Himself through Christ. But notice that the passage goes on to say that having crossed that Bridge and become reconciled to God, God "has [now] committed to us the message of reconciliation. We are therefore Christ's ambassadors, as though God were making his appeal through us" (vv. 19–20).

An ambassador is someone who is sent to represent someone else. Christ's followers are His ambassadors to the world. In other words, once we have surrendered our lives to the lordship of Christ, we no longer represent ourselves; we represent Christ. We are still male or female. We are still "red, brown, yellow, black, [or] white," as the Sunday school chorus says. We are still African American or Native American, or Asian American or Irish American, or Anglo-Saxon American or Latino American, or whatever. Or maybe not American at all, but a member of one of the other nationalities that comprise 95 percent of the world.

But what we look like, where we come from, what language we speak, who our people are—once we cross over the Bridge and enter into a relationship with Christ, no longer does any of that determine whom we will serve with our lives. We now belong to Christ, and whatever may have contributed to our sense of identity in the past is now subordinated to a fundamentally new identity that derived from Him: "If anyone is in Christ, he is a new creation." In short, we are now sons and daughters of the King. Our identity and relationship with the King does not eliminate human distinctions, but it supercedes all human distinctions.

Freed from making our lives all about human distinctions, we are in a position to build bridges of reconciliation, just as 2 Corinthians 5 says. Thanks to Christ, what was formerly impossible—to build bridges across the racial divide—is now very possible.

Very possible, but also very challenging! The nearly twenty-four-mile-long span of the Lake Pontchartrain Causeway took twelve years to build. The Golden Gate Bridge took four years to link San Francisco Peninsula with Marin County. Both required extraordinary engineering, coupled with a lot of expensive resources and dedicated workers who brought energy, focus, and no small amount of bravery. Is there any reason to believe that building bridges of racial reconciliation will take any less? If anything, it will take more. Indeed, it will take the power of God to change hearts. But God does not snap His fingers, as it were, and make racial troubles disappear. As I saw firsthand in Mendenhall, God works mightily, but He never shortchanges the process. Sometimes we may feel that we are waiting on Him, but most of the time I suspect He is waiting on us—to show up and do what He has asked us to do.

A New Community

We've certainly got our work cut out for us. And while there are many problems and many issues concerning racial reconciliation that our society in general needs to address, I want to direct my remarks here squarely at the body of Christ—at those of us who have crossed the Bridge and who claim Christ as Lord. We Christians need to build bridges of reconciliation everywhere, but the place to begin is right inside our own families and church communities. Sadly, we suffer from the same divisions that exist elsewhere in the world. Divisions of doctrine, gender, race and ethnicity, class, politics, and so on. Controversial issues and the problems they entail can cause untold damage among the people of God.

Now to put things in perspective, the kinds of divisions I mentioned have troubled the church since its founding (read Acts 15). And why not? We are all just sinners saved by grace, so we brought our prejudices, ignorance, and other divisive tendencies with us when we came into the faith. But also like the New Testament Christians, and like true believers ever since, we need to heed the teaching of God's Word and remember that He intends for us to overcome all forms of disunity by building bridges in the body of Christ.

To give one of many examples: Paul, in writing to the Colossian Christians, described them as "renewed" (literally *renovated*) people in Christ. As such, he admonished them to "put on the new self, which is being renewed in knowledge in the image of its Creator. Here there is no Greek or Jew, circumcised or uncircumcised, barbarian, Scythian, slave or free, but Christ is all, and is in all" (Col. 3:10–11). So once again, we see that belonging to Christ does not eliminate human distinctions, but it supercedes all human distinctions.

What does that mean in practice? The passage spells it out in black and white:

> Therefore, as God's chosen people, holy and dearly loved, clothe yourselves with compassion, kindness, humility, gentleness and patience. Bear with each other and forgive whatever grievances you may have against one another. Forgive as the Lord forgave you. And over all these virtues put on love, which binds them all together in perfect unity.

Let the peace of Christ rule in your hearts, since as members of one body you were called to peace. And be thankful.
(Col. 3:12–15)

That's what I call a bridge of reconciliation! People being ruled by
who they are in Christ, by who He has made them to be. People
intentionally working, by His power and grace, to bind themselves
together in a perfect bond of unity.

Building Bridges at Home

The first place we Christians need to build those kinds of bridges
of unity is in our families. Did you know that the moment after we
say "I do" at our wedding, we are just as selfish and sinful as we
were before we said "I do"?

Unfortunately, "I do" is no magic formula for change. The
changes happen only if we learn how to build bridges to our spouse.
If we aren't intentionally building bridges, then our marriage will
certainly be in trouble, because a giant gulf is already there. When
there is a division in marriage, we need to learn how it works for
a husband and wife to say to each other, "I was wrong," "I made a
mistake," or "Please forgive me," all of which are phrases that build
bridges instead of making the gulf wider.

The same is true with our children. Parents, we need to build
bridges between ourselves and our children by praying for and with
our children, by seeking to understand our children, and by spending time in developing a relationship with our children.

One of the greatest means of bridge building between a parent
and a child is for the parent to admit a mistake by saying, "I was
wrong. I'm sorry. Please forgive me." That is so hard to do! One
time our family was traveling down to New Orleans for Rosie and

me to speak at an event. On the way, we stopped in Hattiesburg, Mississippi, to eat breakfast. As soon as they brought us our food, my son Ryan, who was quite young at the time, began gobbling down his eggs and bacon just a little too quickly. That caused him to drop some of the food on his nice, clean clothes. That upset me, because I wanted everyone in the family to look good for the event we were going to. So I reached over, squeezed his arm tightly, and said in a very loud and stern voice, "No, son! You need to slow down!"

I went back to eating again. But when I looked up, I saw tears running down Ryan's cheeks. In that moment I realized I had been way too harsh and had squeezed Ryan's arm way too hard. I felt sad for Ryan and disappointed in myself. So when we finished breakfast and were getting back in the car, I stopped and put my arms around my son and said, "Ryan, your daddy is sorry he got so mad. I made a mistake in how I treated you. I was wrong." I wish you could have seen the joy that broke out on little Ryan's face when I told him that! You see, his relationship with his daddy was restored. A bridge had been rebuilt. If I had not taken the time to rebuild that bridge, I would have left a gulf between me and my son.

Building Bridges at Church

The next domain where we Christians desperately need to build bridges is in and among our local churches. The vast majority of churches in the United States are homogeneous—that is, they are filled with people who look pretty much the same. Mostly white or mostly black, or mostly Latino or mostly Korean, or whatever. Now you wouldn't think we'd be divided from people who look a lot like us. But just consider what happens when someone in our church offers, say, a different political opinion than we have. Look out!

A number of years ago I read an excellent book entitled *Why*

America Doesn't Work by Chuck Colson of Prison Fellowship and Jack Eckerd, founder of Eckerd Drugs. After finishing the book, I joked to my staff at The Mendenhall Ministry, "That book almost persuaded me to become a Republican!" They all laughed, but especially my executive vice president at the time, who was a die-hard Republican. I loved giving him a hard time about the effects of his party's policies on poor folks, so I knew he'd love hearing that I was open to the ideas of two well-known conservatives. We had a good laugh about it all.

I didn't fare nearly so well when I was doing a radio show in Dallas one time, and a lady called in and said, "Mr. Weary, I hear what you're saying, and I appreciate what you're doing in your ministry. But I simply don't understand how anybody can vote Democrat and still be a Christian." She was totally sincere! I must say, her comment upset me on many levels. But I replied as calmly as I could, "Ma'am, I've traveled all around this country, and I've spoken in all kinds of different cultural settings. I've come into contact with lots of people who love Jesus and vote Republican. But I've also come into contact with lots of people who love Jesus and vote Democrat. How can you account for that?"

Let me say this about politics when it comes to church: I want to encourage Christians to go out and vote. Vote your convictions. Vote your preferences. Vote your conscience. That's one of the great, fundamental rights that we enjoy as United States citizens, and I believe the Lord calls us to be good citizens—which means exercising our right to vote whenever we have the opportunity.

But just remember that once you've voted and come back to the body of Christ, you are no longer a Republican or Democrat or Independent. You are no longer conservative or liberal or libertarian. You are no longer a Soccer Mom or an urban black or a tax-and-spend liberal or a NASCAR Republican or a Tea Partier. Those are all just labels, and labels are not allowed inside the body of Christ. There, your identity is found in Christ. You are a kingdom person above anything else. And so am I. You and I will not agree on every political issue. But I want to point out that political division is a powerful strategy that Satan is using, now more than ever, to create factions and fissures within the church. That's what happens when we wear our labels to church or put labels on our brothers and sisters in the Lord. The Devil wants to separate believers from one another—the exact opposite of Christ's call to unity. We must resist that temptation to choose sides and condemn other Christians because they are not on "our" side. We need to study up on how to remain kingdom people, devoted to the King above all else.

Building Bridges Between Churches

Well, now, if divisions can exist between people who look a lot like one another, imagine the chasms that open up when we encounter people who don't look at all like us. I experienced that firsthand when I was growing up in Simpson County, Mississippi. There were several white churches in Mendenhall, right across the railroad tracks from my community. They would send missionaries to Africa, but they wouldn't send anyone across the tracks to the Black Quarters. Nor would they let a black person into their church services on Sunday mornings. Think of that: two racially diverse communities living just a few yards apart, with Christians in both communities. Yet those two communities were effectively an entire world apart. How did that show anyone the love and unity that Christ intends for His people?

Thanks to the Civil Rights Act and many other gains over the past fifty years, things have changed substantially in Mendenhall, throughout the South, and throughout the rest of the United States. African Americans in Mendenhall no longer have to fear coming across the tracks to shop or work. I am now able to visit and even preach in white churches where, not that many years ago, I would have been asked to leave.

Yet in many ways, not much has changed. Throughout the country, the Sunday morning worship service is still the most segregated hour of the week. And my points earlier about the beauty and strength of racial and cultural diversity help to explain why. People naturally feel more comfortable with people who are like them. Church-growth experts call that the principle of homogeneity. When we worship God, we prefer to do so in ways that feel natural to us. We want the music, the language, the rituals, the symbols, and the teaching to reflect what our hearts believe and feel. Different racial and cultural groups have different ways of expressing worship, and there's nothing wrong with affiliating with a congregation that fits one's cultural norms.

But there are two big problems with getting too comfortable in a church of people just like us. First, we can start thinking that our group's way of "doing church" is the best way, or even the only way, to worship God. How many times have you found yourself looking at another church's format or style and thinking, "I can't believe they do that!" Meaning that you can't believe "those people" are so vocal and expressive. Surely God can't be pleased with such unruly behavior. Or maybe you can't believe "those people" are so stiff and formal and traditional. Surely God can't be impressed with such empty ritual. Or maybe you can't believe "those people" allow that kind of music. Surely God can't be happy that people are having such a good time.

All of this leads to the second problem, which is worse than the first: as if it's not enough to be suspicious about the way "those people" worship Christ, we allow ourselves to think that we don't need to associate with "those people." We may even go to great lengths to avoid associating with "those people." After all, they don't look like us, they don't think like us, they don't have the same values, they don't have the same problems. What would we have in common? Oh, sure, maybe they call themselves Christians, and maybe in His grace God includes them in His family. But there's nothing going on with them that we need to concern ourselves with. We have our own church, our own needs, our own set of concerns. Let's just ignore "those people."

By means of indulging such indifference in our attitude, we perpetuate the divisions in Christ's body. If you think I'm exaggerating, just look at countless communities across the United States today, whether big cities like Detroit, Chicago, Dallas, or Los Angeles, or small rural towns like the one where I grew up in Mississippi and with which I now work today. In case after case you'll find a divide. It could be a river, an expressway, a highway, or a set of railroad tracks. It may even be an invisible divide. But on one side you'll find affluent people, mostly white, and on the other side you'll find poor people, mostly minorities. And on *both* sides of the divide you'll find Christians and their churches.

It's a rare community where those Christians are going both ways across the divide to build bridges of unity. Yet I believe that's exactly what Christ wants us to do. He doesn't want us to stay hunkered down—or bunkered down—in our homogeneous churches. Don't get me wrong: it's fine to go to our "own" church on most Sunday mornings. But if we are serious about Christ's call to unity, we're going to have to get up and leave our comfort zone and go pay a visit to "those people" across the divide.

Relationships Across the Divide

Which brings me to a question that I am always compelled to ask. Let me warn you first, because this may make you feel uncomfortable: *How many Christians do you know who don't look like you?* Many of us know people in general who don't look like us. We know them from work. We meet them at our children's schools. They transact our business at the bank window. They service our cars. They mow our lawns. They work on our computers. They may even be our physician.

But in this book, I'm especially focused on Christians knowing other Christians who don't look like them. So again: *How many Christians do you know who don't look like you?*

Brothers and sisters, racial reconciliation based on the gospel starts there! We can reach out all day long to people in general who don't look like us. That's fine and that ought to happen. When it does, may we be faithful ambassadors of Christ to those folks. But of all the people who don't look like us, the very first ones with whom we ought to be building bridges of reconciliation are those who, like us, have already crossed the Bridge, so they are now our brothers and sisters in Christ. Let's seek love and unity within that family above all else. Then we'll really have something to talk about with those other people we know who don't look like us.

How can that happen? Well, this is one place where local churches can really play a significant role. Let me challenge pastors and other leaders in local congregations to pick up the phone and contact the pastor of a nearby church that is filled with folks who don't look like yours. Tell him that God has been speaking to your heart about building bridges between groups of Christians, and you'd like to take a first step toward that by the two of you meeting for breakfast or lunch. You might suggest some neutral location. Other than that, have no agenda. I might also suggest that you send him a copy of this book ahead of time, so you have a common framework for conversation.

The purpose of that initial get-together is to launch the first tiny strand across the divide that will hopefully grow into a strong cable and eventually become a bunch of strong cables that can support an entire bridge of reconciliation between two groups of Christians. Perhaps that initial meeting will turn into a handful of visits to the other church by folks from your congregation and vice versa. Perhaps it will lead to the other pastor coming to preach in your pulpit or vice versa. Perhaps it will lead to a shared worship service, with both congregations joining together to compare how much they share in Christ as well as to highlight and celebrate the different ways they express themselves to God.

Of course, one of the most important things that reaching out like that can accomplish is to introduce Christians from your church to Christians who don't look like them. Out of those interactions may grow new relationships, especially if the two groups go through shared experiences together, like service projects or joint worship services.

Praying Together, Partnering Together

So does this mean that racial reconciliation boils down to churches from different groups eating lots of meals together and occasionally sampling each other's music? Is that all we have to do to be able to mark racial reconciliation off our to-do list? Absolutely not! The reason Christians from different backgrounds need to build bridges to each other is because Jesus has plans for us to start working together. In Ephesians 4:12, Paul clearly says that church leaders are supposed to "equip" (that is, prepare or ready) God's people for what he calls "the work of service," which is about "building up the body of Christ" (NASB). In other words, the Lord has a building project underway. His people are the workers on that project.

So what does that look like in practice? One key part of it is that Christ wants His people to do kingdom work right in their own communities. And He wants the Christians from *all* the groups in those communities to participate in that work.

I know what that could have and should have looked like in Mendenhall when I was growing up. I've already described how the white churches stayed on their side of the tracks, and the black churches stayed on their side of the tracks. They let the system of segregation determine the nature and scope of their mission. But if the churches at that time had followed Ephesians 4, leaders from *both* the white churches and the black churches (those were the only two groups in Simpson County at the time) would have come together, first to declare their unity in Christ and then to consider what kingdom work Jesus might have in mind for them in the community of Mendenhall. I suspect that some of the pressing issues in the Black Quarters might have been part of that work.

By the grace of God, the kind of bridge building I've just described is beginning to happen in countless communities across Mississippi. More and more church leaders are taking their first baby steps to launch a thread or two across racial and ethnic divides. Praise God for that!

But now, let me interject a word of counsel to anyone who is trying to be obedient to God by building those bridges: *don't start with a plan; start with a prayer.* That's what we learned at Mission Mississippi. That's what other Christians have learned in doing this work. The very first and most important thing Christians who don't look like each other ought to do is to start praying together.

That's right, a good old-fashioned prayer meeting! If we have to meet at a neutral site first, so be it. But let's get all the pastors and lay leaders and everyone who is serious about racial reconciliation in the same room, and let's get on our knees before God. Let's start out by praising Him together. And okay, someone is already going to start feeling uncomfortable when the gentleman sitting next to him starts punctuating the prayers with "Amen!" and "Thank you, Jesus!" But is that so bad? Maybe that discomfort is leading to a new awareness and a new respect for someone else's experience with God.

But then let's do some confessing of our sins. I understand; that could really get uncomfortable. So maybe we just start by acknowledging that as the people of God we are divided. We have not pursued the unity for which Christ pleaded to His Father on the night before He laid down His life. Let's own up, before God and before those from whom we've been estranged, that we have not been diligent to override the pressures of our society to keep things separate, to keep people at enmity with each other, to keep the dysfunctional systems of power and control in place, to keep things as they are.

If we are really brave, we might even confess and own our own personal prejudices, ignorance, and fears. This is a work of the Lord Jesus through the power of the Holy Spirit in our hearts that produces awareness of these sins and the courage to confess them as such. After having confessed our sinfulness and brokenness, we can celebrate the hope we have in the cross of Christ, which paid for our sins and bridges the distance between us and a holy, righteous God by extending forgiveness. And then we can start extending forgiveness to one another for past hurts, wrongs, injustices, misunderstandings, and the like.

Only after all of that are we ready to ask the key question, *Lord, what would you have us do?* "Us" is the operative word. You see, unless we have come together as brothers and sisters in Christ—apart from labels, apart from political affiliations, apart from theological traditions, apart from racial and cultural distinctions—the word "us" has no meaning. "Us" only has regard before the Lord when it means *"all* of us." Because our King has no interest in leading an army with disunity in the ranks.

During the past thirty years, I've been called in as a consultant to many a group of concerned Christians who want to "do something" about the terrible problems their communities are facing. Sometimes there has already been a lot of planning and a lot of discussion about what "ought" to happen and how to "make" it happen. But as we learned in the early goings of Mission Mississippi, all of those good intentions will likely go nowhere until those involved have come to grips with three vital questions: (1) Have we included the leaders of the folks we intend to "help" in our discussions and planning? (2) Have we prayed first? By which I mean not just customary prayers to kick off a meeting, but intensive, lengthy, and focused sessions devoted to prayer, along the lines I just described above. And (3) what does God already seem to be doing in the community, quite apart from anything we've done? Where is He already at work? How can we cooperate with that, instead of charging off in a whole new direction?

If you are exercised about some thorny problem in your community, or if you feel burdened about some community near yours that is struggling with thorny problems—praise God for that! It indicates that the Lord is working in your heart. But now consider this: God cares about that situation a whole lot more than you do. The fact that He has stirred up your heart to care shows that He is summoning His people to address that concern. But guess what?

The people who are actually in the middle of that situation likely feel even more concern than you do. At the least, they know more about what's going on there than you do. And the odds are good that some of them are Christians. Consider that God may be calling you to *partner* with those Christians to discover together what He plans to do about their situation. That's how God works among His people.

Real-World Bridges

What does it actually look like for Christians from different groups to partner together in kingdom work? It might mean any one or more of the examples of bridge building that follow:

- A tutoring program to help children learn to read, the goal being to get them into high school (a child who drops out before high school is essentially doomed to a life of poverty and/or prison), and to show that Jesus cares about children.
- A Little League baseball team, the goal being to give boys a healthy experience of teamwork, competition, winning and losing, and strong male role models, and to show that Jesus cares about boys becoming men.
- A group of Christians "taking over" a public school during a long weekend and completely refurbishing it with new paint, repaired windows and doors, cleaned rooms, organized supplies, mowed grass and other landscaping, working light fixtures, and other improvements, the goal being to revitalize the educational environment for the students, and to show that Jesus cares about the education of youth.
- A group of Christian lawyers meeting personally on a pro bono basis with individuals and couples to discuss their legal

issues and explain options, the goal being to provide crucial guidance and counsel, and to show that Jesus cares about justice.

- A program to help men coming out of prison gain a skill, get a job, develop a work ethic, assimilate back into society, and earn an honest wage, and to show that Jesus cares about workers and their work.
- A group of Christian businesspeople birthing a business that generates new jobs for people who have been unemployed, the goal being to feed families, provide people with dignity, and transform a local economy, and to show that Jesus cares about supplying people's material needs.
- A day camp during the summer, the goal being to give children a safe place to spend their day, a chance to feed them a healthy meal, and an opportunity to tell them about Jesus, to show that Jesus wants to be their Savior and Friend.
- A group of Christians meeting with the mayor and city council to ask them for one practical thing that their group can do to serve the community, the goal being to serve the community, and to show that Jesus cares about communities.

All of these ideas have actually happened. Real Christians who don't look like each other have actually partnered together in these ways to bring the love of Christ and the good news of His kingdom to their local communities. The possibilities for other kinds of engagement are endless.

When Christians who don't look like each other come together like that, three powerful things happen: (1) they actually address a real need in their community; (2) they *show* the world what racial reconciliation looks like, by coming together as brothers and sisters in Christ and living out the unity that Christ desires; and (3) because of that unity they offer a very compelling witness to the world that Jesus is Lord of a united people such that the world may know and believe that the Father sent His Son and has truly loved His people even as the Father loved His Son—the very thing Jesus prayed for in John 17. Imagine that—we can be the answer to a prayer that Jesus prayed!

And oh, how we need to be that answer! Because our world is so divided. Several years ago, television journalist Diane Sawyer asked the Reverend Billy Graham, "If you could wave your hand and make one problem in this world go away, what would it be?" Without a moment's hesitation, Dr. Graham replied, "Racial division and strife."

Only one hand is powerful enough to make racial division and strife go away. That's the nail-scarred hand of Jesus. When He stretched out His arms on the cross and submitted to being executed, He laid down a Bridge to reconcile human beings with God. But in doing so, He also made a way for those who cross that Bridge to build bridges of reconciliation with others. What He did, He now calls us to do: "He has committed to us the message of reconciliation. We are therefore Christ's ambassadors" (2 Cor. 5:19–20).

So who are some Christians you know who don't look like you?

CHAPTER 9

"Thank You, America!"

Earlier in the book, I told about the impossible dream that God brought about in helping us raise up the Genesis One Christian School at The Mendenhall Ministries. In the beginning it seemed impossible, because all we had was an abandoned schoolhouse, the vacant shell of Harper High. That eyesore only served to remind every black person in town of an earlier dream that had died out. It was a visible symbol of that persistent mind-set: *nothing is ever going to change.*

My coworkers and I determined to replace that mind-set with a brand new mind-set that leaned away from the idea that "all" we had was an abandoned building, or even that "all" we had was faith. Instead, our foundation was: *above all else, we have God!* And our God is the God of the impossible. We can trust Him to do what only He can do. He can transform empty buildings into thriving classrooms. He can transform children with no hope into educated, productive citizens who have purpose and a sense of calling to their lives.

That's why I used to walk by the Genesis One Christian School every day, after it was up and running, and give thanks to God for bringing that miracle about. Then I'd pray for the children in that school—children who, thanks to what God had done, were growing up with a much better opportunity to learn than I ever had at their age. As I thought about their futures, I'd pray, "Lord, make these children into something! Make them lawyers and doctors, scientists and professors, businesspeople and ministers, homemakers and missionaries!" And the more I thought about what those kids could become, I decided to throw in another "impossible" dream: "And Lord, why not make one of them *a president!*"

An Answer to My Prayer

On November 4, 2008, God began to answer that prayer with the election of Barack Obama as the forty-fourth president of the United States, the first African American to hold that office.

Now let me say right away, I know a lot of folks who view the election of Barack Obama as anything but an answer to prayer, especially those whose politics differ significantly from Mr. Obama's. But if you're a follower of Christ, and if, as Paul instructed followers of Christ to do, you pray for rulers and all who are in authority (see 1 Tim. 2:2), then even though you may disagree with Obama's politics and policies, you must at least concede that God sovereignly placed him into office. Because it is God who establishes rulers and removes rulers (see Dan. 2:21).

For me and for countless African Americans, the election of Barack Obama was another impossible dream come true. There have been many watershed moments in race relations in our country's history, events that we now look back on and say, "That was a milestone. That changed things. The races acted differently toward each other after that." Things like the Emancipation Proclamation. The adoption of the Thirteenth Amendment to the Constitution, outlawing slavery. The 1954 *Brown v. Board of Education* decision on segregation. The 1963 Civil Rights March in Washington, DC, where Dr. Martin Luther King Jr. gave his "I Have a Dream" speech. The Civil Rights Act of 1964.

The election of Barack Obama in 2008 was one more of those watershed moments in our country's racial history.

A lot of people would say that this was because Obama was the first African American to actually win a presidential election. That was certainly a notable achievement. But what made his election a watershed was that Obama didn't run for office as an African American. He ran for office as a man who unapologetically wanted to become our president because he believed he could serve the country. He didn't run as a victim or as the first African American. He presented the face of someone who spoke to *all* the electorate because he wanted to be their president. He just happened to be an African American.

For the most part, he stayed away from discussions of race during his campaign. However, he was forced to address the issue in the aftermath of some highly controversial statements delivered from the pulpit by his pastor, the Reverend Jeremiah Wright. In response, Obama gave a marvelous speech in Philadelphia in which he brilliantly juxtaposed what is both the worst and the best about this country when it comes to race relations:

> The profound mistake of Reverend Wright's sermons is not that he spoke about racism in our society. It's that he spoke as if our society was static; as if no progress has been made; as if this country—a country that has made it possible for

one of his own members to run for the highest office in the
land and build a coalition of white and black, Latino and
Asian, rich and poor, young and old—is still irrevocably
bound to a tragic past. But what we know—what we have
seen—is that America can change. That is the true genius of
this nation. What we have already achieved gives us hope—
the audacity to hope—for what we can and must achieve
tomorrow.[1]

That speech, along with his performances in the three presidential debates and on the campaign trail, showed Obama to be an
articulate person who had to be taken seriously. He could answer
the questions of the day as an American, period. That made him
electable. And then, when he did get elected, the fact that he was
an African American sent vibes throughout the country to every
African American, Latino American, Asian American, and every
other person in the minority, and the message was: "I live in the
United States, where supposedly everyone is created equal. Well,
it's really true, because someone of any race can grow up and be
president." And so a person whose goal was not to break a barrier
but to get elected, ended up not only getting elected but breaking a
barrier. That was a major milestone!

Equal Opportunity at the White House

Perhaps no one articulated the meaning of that milestone more
eloquently than author and poet Maya Angelou, who was interviewed by CBS's Harry Smith the morning after Barack Obama's

---

1. Senator Barack Obama, "A More Perfect Union" (televised speech, National
Constitution Center; Philadelphia, PA, March 18, 2008), https://my.barackobama
.com/page/content/hisownwords.

election. Her joy literally overcame her capacity for words: "I'm so proud, and filled, I can hardly talk without weeping. I'm so filled with pride for my country. What do you say? We are growing up! My God, I'm so grateful. . . . I mean, look at our souls, look at our hearts. *We* have elected a black man to talk for us, to speak for us! *We*—blacks, whites, Asians, Spanish-speaking, Native Americans—*we* have done it! Fat, thin, pretty, plain . . . —*we* have done it! My Lord, I am an American, baby!" She was bursting with excitement.

Smith then asked her, "Why this man?" Angelou replied, "Because he's intelligent, Harry. I don't mean intellectually clever. I mean intelligent. I mean what used to be called 'mother wit.' He has common sense, which is, I'm sorry to say, most uncommon. Because he knows that together, we can be somebody. You see? And he is inclusive as opposed to exclusive. I know that he knows he is the president of *every* black person, *every* white person. He's [even] the president of the bigots. And he must remember that."[2] Wise words!

When America woke up on November 5, 2008, a major shift had taken place. It was no longer a nation where only a white man could be the leader. There was now a door of equal opportunity even at the White House. That's huge! That begins to change a mind-set. It creates a model for every person of color, that the system can work—even if pockets in that system remain locked in a racist past.

During the election, a lot of my white friends would ask, "Dolphus, there's no way I can vote for Barack Obama. Does that make me a racist?"

Great question! I told them, "If you've been voting conservative Republican all your life, and you disagree with Barack Obama's

---

2. Maya Angelou, interview by Harry Smith, *The Early Show*, CBS, November 5, 2008, http://www.cbsnews.com/video/watch/?id=4574386n.

platform, and you vote for someone else, that's fine. That does not make you a racist. But now if you've been a lifelong Democrat and always voted for a Democrat to be the president, and you like Obama's platform, but the only reason you would not vote for him is because he's an African American, then yes, that's racist."

The great news about Obama's election is that it showed that a convincing majority of Americans could look past race and see the person, listen to his ideas, and decide to vote for him based on what he stood for, not on the color of his skin. That was a watershed. It proved that Americans finally believe a black man is capable of being a leader in every facet of this country.

Pray for Your President

Of course, it doesn't help that he had to become the president at one of the worst times in our country's history. He promised to bring change, and certainly a lot of changes are needed. But change always carries a heavy price tag. So on the one hand, the expectations on him are sky-high. Yet on the other hand, the problems he's inherited with the economy and terrorism and the wars in Iraq and Afghanistan and so forth are so unprecedented that he's sailing in uncharted waters. That's why I say that we ought to be praying for him regardless. Whether or not you voted for him and whether or not you agree with his policies, every Christian ought to be praying for Barack Obama, along with all of our other leaders, every single day. First Timothy 2:1–2 sets forth this Christian responsibility in plain language. It's simply something God says we need to do. Are you praying, Christian?

Another thing we Christians can do, of course, is to seize this moment as an opportunity to work as never before toward racial reconciliation based on the gospel. Obama's election opened up a whole new chance to dialogue about race in this country. And in fact, it created a bit of a window for talking about racial and ethnic issues around the world. America is in the spotlight. The world is looking at us a little differently than it ever has before. And here's why: because a man whose father is from Africa is now the leader of the free world. And he got there because the people of America put him there. Can you even imagine the message of hope that sends to people everywhere!

Obama's election by no means solves all of America's problems with race and ethnicity. Far from it! Nor does it mean anyone has to agree with all the decisions he makes or how he runs the country. He has to prove himself, just like any other president. If his programs aren't to the people's liking, there's an electoral process to deal with that.

But I do believe that America has changed in regard to race as a result of electing an African American as president. What's changed is the perception that America will never change. The election proves, yes it can, yes it is, and yes it will.

That's why I said at the beginning of this chapter that God *began* to answer my prayer that someday a child from Genesis One Christian School could become president. He hasn't completely answered it yet. But now we know for certain that it's not impossible. Only a very short time ago, it did seem impossible. But never, never, ever forget: *above all else, we have God!* And our God is the God of the impossible. He can change a person. He can change a community. He can change a nation. He *will* change the world!

CHAPTER 10

Making It R.E.A.L.

In the aftermath of Reggie's death in 2004, the board of Mission Mississippi graciously gave me six weeks off to deal with the situation, grieve with my family, and take some initial steps in trying to recover from that tragic loss. I will always be grateful to those men and women for that time. I don't know how I would have been able to continue without it.

When I finally did return to my work, I learned that my close friend Neddie Winters had been serving as the interim executive director in my absence, at the request of the board. Neddie was a board member, and he was also the pastor of Voice of Calvary Church in Jackson, a sister congregation to Mendenhall Bible Church, where Rosie and I are members. Neddie was doing a fantastic job leading the organization. I found him deeply immersed in strategic planning, setting goals, developing the staff, and so many other key projects. In fact, things were running so well that Mission Mississippi didn't really need Dolphus!

And that's when a light went on for me. What did I really *want* to do with my life going forward? What did I really have the energy to do?

I've learned since that a profound loss like I'd gone through has a way of confronting a person with what really matters to him or her. Part of it is that losing someone close to you has a way of putting life into perspective. Each of us is only on this earth for a brief moment in time. So you want to make your life count. That leads into another part of it, which is that it takes so much energy to process the grief and get going again with your life that you don't have any energy left over for peripheral matters. You quickly find that the only things worth putting energy into are things that give you energy back.

All of that thinking forced the question: What should I *really* be doing with my life? What were my core gifts? And what did I care about the most? As I took stock, I realized that running an organization was great stuff, but it was not me. I'm a motivator, an encourager, and a bridge builder. That's who I am. That's what brings me joy. That's what fits me.

So I went to the board and told them, "Guys, I think Dolphus Weary has brought some good gifts to this work. But now, in this new season of life, I would rather concentrate on the things I enjoy the most and at which I feel I'm the most effective. I look at the outstanding job Neddie has been doing in running this ministry in my absence. That's stuff I can do, but I don't love doing it. He does. I recommend you hire Neddie to run Mission Mississippi, and let Dolphus stick to preaching, teaching, encouraging, and motivating. That's what I do best, and I can handle that emotionally."

The board agreed, and they adopted my recommendation. Once again, I was so grateful for how they treated me.

A Heart for the Rural Poor

My new arrangement with Mission Mississippi allowed me to devote more energy to a foundation that Rosie and I had formed earlier called R.E.A.L. Christian Foundation. R.E.A.L. stands for Rural Education and Leadership, because education and leadership are the foundations on which real, lasting gains can be established for poor, rural Mississippi communities like the one in which I grew up.

When I left The Mendenhall Ministries in 1997, the only thing that really changed for Rosie and me was where I would carry out my calling. We still had a heart for the rural poor. The question was how we would do that. In 1998, I became the head of Mission Mississippi because I was fully committed to the process of racial reconciliation. But how could I lead in that effort and still reach out to the rural poor? R.E.A.L. Christian Foundation was our answer to that question.

The seeds of R.E.A.L. were sown way back in my formative years by John Perkins. Both through exhortation and example, he stressed that everyone should always have a vision for life that is larger than oneself. I never forgot that.

Years later, when I was president of TMM and was asked to serve on the World Vision Board, I had the opportunity to listen to the story of World Vision through the eyes of Betty Wagner. Betty was an assistant with Bob Pierce, World Vision's president at the time. She talked about how World Vision had become a large, looming organization with work all over the world. But despite being everywhere, it could not do everything. And so World Vision had learned to come alongside many smaller ministry organizations and groups of Christians around the world to help them do what they were called to do and in fact were doing better than World Vision could, because these smaller ministries were focused on a single area. World Vision could leverage its strength and resources to make those smaller ministries much more effective.

Following her time at World Vision, Betty went on to start Wayfarers Ministries in California, which funds the special and emergency needs of missionaries, pastors, Bible students, and Christian schools throughout the world. When I saw Betty's organization getting behind people doing important things in small, out-of-the-way places, I thought, "That's what I want to do! I want to come alongside all the tiny little ministries in Mississippi that are doing good work in the name of Christ among the rural poor."

And then I came across a guy already working with rural churches in Mississippi. A major foundation would give him a grant every year, and out of that money he would issue $500 and $750 checks to support summer programs designed to reach out to young people. He was having a great impact. The only problem was that every year, he had to wait on that foundation to decide whether it was going to keep funding the program, and if so, how much money it was going send. As I reflected on that model, I thought, "Wouldn't it be better if folks in Mississippi somehow had their own endowment, rather than having to wait on whether some foundation far away will come through or not?"

John Perkins, Betty Wagner, the guy passing out small foundation grants—all of those influences were working together on my mind right about the time Rosie and I left TMM. A vision was becoming clear to start a foundation to support ministries working with the rural poor in Mississippi.

Two Thousand Books and No Money

But where would we get the initial seed funding? John Perkins had used the proceeds from his books to start a foundation aimed at urban work. I reasoned that maybe I should do the same with my book *I Ain't Comin' Back*. In fact, there was about $100,000 from sales of that book available right about that time. Historically, I had donated those proceeds to fund scholarships at the Genesis One Christian School. But maybe now that I was leaving, I could switch those funds to start up R.E.A.L., and that money could be put to different purposes.

It was Rosie who put her foot down on that idea and said I would do no such thing! Whatever money had been raised for Genesis One kids needed to go to Genesis One kids. To pull it out now would mean lots of kids not being able to go to school in the fall. That wouldn't be right, would it?

"No," I agreed. "But I hate thinking there's $100,000 sitting there, and I have to leave it there."

"Dolphus," she shot back, "if God used something you wrote to raise up $100,000 once, He can do it again." I couldn't argue with that.

In the end, we worked out an arrangement with TMM board that whatever monies had been raised to-date from the sale of *I Ain't Comin' Back* would stay with TMM. Going forward, I would retain the rights to the book and be free to use any new monies generated from book sales as I saw fit. The board responded well to the challenge of finding new sources of scholarship money for the Genesis One school. And I started R.E.A.L. Christian Foundation—with two thousand books and no money!

I had no doubt that I could sell those books. Why, I'd spent twenty years selling those books! Still, I'd have to sell a lot of books to come anywhere near my dream of getting the foundation's endowment up to $1 million. I was concerned too that most of the people I would be talking to across the country had already bought copies of the book. I couldn't just sell them the same old book. In fact, a lot of them were already asking me, "When's your next book coming out? We loved the story of what God did in bringing you back to Mississippi and working at TMM. But that was twenty years ago. What's the rest of the story?" That demand for a "sequel" is largely what motivated me to start working on this book.

Another financial pressure I was facing was how to pay for my kids' college educations. While Rosie and I had savings, we didn't have anywhere near the kind of money it would take to afford college for our kids. Yet we believed strongly in the value of education. Where was the money for that education going to come from? We easily could have used the proceeds from the book, and no one would have thought twice about it. Some people might even have argued that having the book back was God's way of providing for that need. But Rosie and I felt a strong conviction to stay dedicated to the idea that any money coming in from the book should go toward rural poor people. I recalled Rosie's steadfast trust that God could provide the money to start R.E.A.L.: If God did it once, He can do it again. And so I decided He could also provide money for college tuitions.

And He did! He provided for all of those needs beyond what any of us could have expected. I've already told the story of how He worked in Danita's situation to afford an education at Rhodes. And Reggie's costs at Tougaloo were also covered. As for R.E.A.L., I watched God work in marvelous ways as I traveled around the country speaking—always careful to take a box of books with me. The books continued to sell. People got excited about the vision for R.E.A.L. and donated gifts of all sizes.

When Reggie died in 2004, we started the Reggie Weary Memorial Scholarship Fund, as I mentioned earlier. It's a fund within the larger R.E.A.L. Foundation that provides scholarships for poor, rural African-American young people in Mississippi. We also created the Katherine Weathersby Memorial Scholarship Fund in honor of a TMM board member who was killed in a car accident in 2003. That fund is designed to help parents with children at the Genesis One school pay their portion of the tuition when they are experiencing unusual hardship.

The endowment for R.E.A.L. reached $1 million in 2006. That was an amazing thing, because my capacity to go out and find funding after Reggie died was severely hampered. But God is always able to do what we can't do, and even what we think can't be done. And so it was one of the happiest moments of my life to be able to stand up at the end of one of the R.E.A.L. Foundation celebration dinners in 2006 and announce that we had reached $1 million. What a proud moment that was! But also a humbling moment. I wanted to make sure that everyone understood full well that Dolphus Weary had not brought in that money—God provided that money! It was one more "impossible" dream that God had brought to pass. There have been so many of those in my life. Once again, God had shown me and everyone else that He is able. His power is sufficient. His faithfulness is trustworthy. His provision is abundant. He can do it—not on our timetable, but on His timetable. It was a joyful celebration that night!

As of the writing of this book, R.E.A.L. Christian Foundation has more than $1.2 million in the general endowment. Our dream over the next five years is to raise it to $5 million.

Small Grants, Big Impact

By law and by design, we give away at least 5 percent of earnings every year in grants to individuals and groups doing ministry among the rural poor in Mississippi. Initially, our grants were in the range of $500 to $1,000. Today, our minimum grant is $1,000, and the maximum is $5,000. We prefer to fund people on an annual basis, because we want to walk alongside ministries for the long-term. At the end of the grant-cycle year, we generally ask the ministries to submit applications for any additional money they believe they need. That gives them an opportunity to send in special requests.

Some people may wonder what good a grant of $500 or $1,000 will do. That doesn't seem like very much money. Can it really make any difference? Indeed it can!

Let me tell you the story of Tony Duckworth. While I was at TMM, one of our key leaders was Timothy Keys, who ended up succeeding me as the president of TMM. Timothy used to have a street ministry in a tiny little town south of Mendenhall called Mount Olive. Tony Duckworth heard the gospel and got saved through that street ministry. He and his wife followed Timothy back to Mendenhall and worked with us in the Pastors Development Program. But God kept his heart alive for the people in Mount Olive. He wanted to see the kinds of things God was doing in Mendenhall start to happen in his hometown.

So about fifteen years ago, Tony began reaching out to the people in Mount Olive. Because of my experience in Mendenhall, I served as something of a mentor to him as he was getting things started. When we set up R.E.A.L. in 1999, Tony and his wife were among the first people to receive a grant. They had a small after-school tutoring program, and R.E.A.L. gave them $500 for materials to use in that program. Then they started a mentoring program for boys, and they received another $500. They started a sports camp, and again R.E.A.L. got behind that. They got that sports camp up

to five or six hundred kids, and they just kept winning those kids
to the Lord.

Then they found that most of the churches nearby didn't want
to deal with the former gang members and the bad kids they were
leading to Christ. So about ten years ago, they started a church.
Tony now pastors that church and is running a ministry. He's doing
a phenomenal job of reaching out and bringing in volunteer groups
to refurbish houses and such. Needless to say, R.E.A.L. is very excited about investing year after year in a person who is that effective.

So can $500 make a difference? Absolutely! Give a small amount
of money to someone doing something effective on a small scale,
and over time their work can grow into something that makes a big
difference on a much larger scale. But it's not the size that matters.
It's the effectiveness.

A similar story could be told about the folks who, like Tony, had
an after-school tutoring program. They had volunteers and people
to do the work, but they didn't have money to buy the materials.
R.E.A.L. gave a grant of $500 to help them buy the materials for
the program. They also used it to buy snacks for the kids, many of
whom were not getting enough food at home. So after the first year,
their grant was increased to $1,000. Today, R.E.A.L. gives them
$5,000 annually, and they're helping lots and lots of children suc-
ceed in school and not fall behind.

Sometimes R.E.A.L. gives a one-time grant for a special project. For instance, TMM had a situation where seventeen boys were
living in a boarding house that had no recreational activities. The
coach who was overseeing them sent in a grant request for $1,500
to buy some recreational equipment and to set up a multimedia library with videos, CDs, and so forth. R.E.A.L. helped him pull that
off so he could work with those boys more effectively.

Another situation was the help R.E.A.L. gave to a school where the budget for the teachers had been cut. The teachers were not making much to begin with, but with the cuts they had to start paying for their own lunches. A $500 gift enabled the teachers to get a hot meal every day.

Another group wanted to take kids from their community to a camp. They requested and received $1,000 to make that possible.

Then there was the sports ministry that was trying to introduce kids to organized sports. But they couldn't transport them around the area because the bus had broken down. R.E.A.L. gave them an emergency gift of $1,000 to get the bus up and running again, so they could carry on with that ministry.

A Ministry of Multiplication

Sometimes the foundation makes grants to projects that are just trying to get started. One of those involved a teacher at the Genesis One Christian School who lived in Morton, Mississippi. It says a lot about her that she was willing to drive forty miles a day to teach in a grade school. But the most exciting thing was that after teaching at Genesis One for eight or nine years, she wanted to start a school in Morton, the small community east of Jackson where she had grown up. So she left Genesis One and started small by putting together an after-school program in Morton.

R.E.A.L. got behind her with a $1,000 grant that first year. Now it's grown into a complete grade school, from nursery through sixth grade, plus the after-school program. It has a wonderful reputation for being the kind of school that welcomes kids who are having difficulty and bringing them along in their math and reading levels. R.E.A.L. gives that school $4,000 a year, and whatever the total investment has been, it's nothing compared to the benefits that have been brought to the people around Morton. It's an island of hope for kids in that county.

One of my favorite stories is about a young lady who is with Young Life in the Mississippi Delta (the northwest section of the state between the Mississippi and Yazoo rivers). She lives in Greenwood but drives twenty-five miles south to Tchula to work with high school girls there. She's got about fifty or sixty girls and boys in her ministry. She herself got pregnant at age fifteen and chose to have the baby. By God's grace she came to Christ, and today she has a heart for rescuing girls from that same trap of immediate gratification.

One of the best things she does is to take those girls to Young Life camps. Imagine kids from Tchula, Mississippi (pop. 2,332) going to a Young Life camp and getting their eyes opened to what is possible for their lives! And so R.E.A.L. is currently funding her work annually with $4,000. She called me one day and said, "You know, Dolphus, R.E.A.L. is the largest single supporter I have that is African American. I've got some white supporters who give more, but among African Americans, y'all are number one."

You have no idea how blessed I was to hear that! Not about being number one, as if there's a competition on, but seeing the dream of R.E.A.L. Christian Foundation doing what we'd hoped and prayed it could do. When I was growing up in poverty in Mendenhall, sweating to death chopping cotton in the summers and huddling next to my brothers and sisters to stay warm in the winters, I never in my wildest dreams could have imagined running a million-dollar foundation that was set up to bring God's love to poor folk like my family. I felt like I was trapped in a hopeless situation. But God reached down and brought John Perkins into my life, and through him, I met Jesus. Now here I am all these years later, able to come alongside another person in similar circumstances, just as

John had with me, and make it possible for her to introduce young people to Jesus. I take so much satisfaction in that and in knowing how much that Young Life leader delights in what she is doing.

One more story: R.E.A.L. helps support a guy who works with athletes in Lexington, Mississippi, just a little south, not too far from Tchula. He calls his organization the Lexington Colts. He starts with youngsters six years old and up, organizing them into football and baseball teams. They go around the area and play other community teams. He's built a whole dimension of spiritual impact into his program, and he follows the kids and keeps tracking with them as they grow up and get into higher-level sports. Recently, he was celebrating the fact that two of his guys are now starters in their respective sports at Jackson State University.

When I heard that, I told him, "Man, that's fantastic! I'm so proud of you! But let me tell you, what's really going to get us excited is when one of those kids you're working with catches the vision of being another Dolphus Weary—someone who was reached in the community, went away to school, and then was willing to come back and reach others." I said that because Lexington is the county seat of Holmes County, one of the poorest counties in the United States. There is so much hopelessness there. But, thank God, the Lexington Colts are providing hope! It's another case of someone doing effective work on a small scale, trusting God to take his five loaves and two fishes and multiply it beyond anything anyone could imagine.

One reason why the Lexington Colts ministry and so many others like it are getting the job done is that they have taken the long view. They are not just looking for the quick fix. One of the problems in our culture is that when a crisis happens, everyone gets all worked up to find out "what went wrong" and then fix it. We want our problems to go away quickly. But as I've said repeatedly, when it comes to poverty you have to look back fifty years or more to discover what has led to the problems we have today. When it comes to poverty, you're dealing with a mind-set and the dysfunctions of a broken system. You can't just introduce a program and change those factors overnight.

Whatever took decades and generations to produce today's problems may take decades and generations to turn around. The people R.E.A.L. supports by and large recognize that. They are committed for the long haul.

Effectiveness Through Excellence

You'll notice that effectiveness is a key value for how R.E.A.L. determines whom to fund. To foster the effectiveness of our grantees, we hold training exercises twice a year. We bring all the groups together at a central place and teach them best practices in things like how to manage their money, how to measure their results, how to network with others, and especially how to partner with other groups doing work similar to theirs.

We've also put in place systems of accountability so we can monitor how people are doing in their ministries and make sure they are using the grant money for the purposes for which it was given. That's a healthy discipline to practice, because we learned early on that when it gets close to the time for reviewing the work and getting revved up for the next funding cycle, people have a tendency to get everything looking good—maybe even a whole lot better than things actually are. We certainly want things to look good. But we're more interested in knowing what's really going on and where the ministries need help.

One of the greatest assets R.E.A.L. has to work with is the outstanding model of The Mendenhall Ministry. It was always our dream for TMM to serve as a model for other ministries. Now that dream has come to pass beyond our expectations. You see, TMM is a great example of someone (John Perkins) coming in and starting small, working faithfully over time, raising up leaders like me and others, and then in God's timing seeing all of the prayer and work and sacrifice and intentionality and faith bear fruit. What began as a simple outreach to young people who had no hope is now a thriving, vital organization with diverse ministries led by third-generation leadership.

Like any ministry, TMM has its ups and downs, its strengths and weaknesses, its opportunities and challenges. But it's got a wonderful history of more than forty years of effectiveness. That makes it invaluable to the vision that R.E.A.L. is trying to instill in all of the ministries we support around the state that are trying to make a difference. Some of them are tiny start-ups being led by people wondering whether they'll make it. Others have great aspirations, never mind their size. For all of them, it's invaluable to be able to point to TMM and say, "Look what God can do! Stay faithful. Stay focused. Trust the Lord's timing. Do not despise small beginnings."

Never Say *Just!*

As near as I can tell, R.E.A.L. seems to be unique in Mississippi in its focus on ministries to the rural poor. Certainly, there are lots of different people working with the rural poor in communities around the state. Most of them are individual efforts, and many of them are doing great work. But I'm not aware of any other foundations, certainly not of our size, dedicated to addressing rural poverty from a Christian perspective.

There was a time when *none* of the ministries and resources I've described in this book existed. Not one! There was just a hopeless situation in Simpson County, Mississippi. Then there was a time when it was just John Perkins and his family, working with a bunch of poor black kids in Mendenhall. They endured a lot of trouble as a result of "not knowing their place" and "stirring things up" in the Black Quarters. Then there was a time when it was just Dolphus Weary and his family and a handful of coworkers, after John moved back to Jackson. We didn't have any health clinic or law office, or Genesis One school or thrift store, or farm or much else. All we had was a call from the Lord to come back to Mississippi. And then there was a time too when we didn't have a million-dollar foundation, just a bunch of books.

But you have to beware of the word *just*. Watch out when someone says "just John Perkins" or "just Dolphus and his family," or "just a bunch of books" or "just an after-school tutoring program," or "just a Young Life group" or "just a sports ministry," or "just a young pastor" or "just a teenager," or "just a black kid from some little place nobody heard of in rural Mississippi." Especially be careful when you find yourself saying "just me." Things that seem "just" too insignificant to matter have a way of becoming *just the things God uses!*

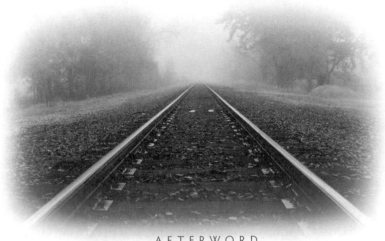

The 300 Club

So how do we plan to grow the endowment for R.E.A.L. Christian Foundation from $1.2 million to $5 million over the next five years? One strategy we've devised is to create The 300 Club. In the Old Testament, God's people the Israelites were oppressed by a nation called the Midianites. The Midianites would wait until harvest time and then invade Israel, carrying off their livestock, stripping the crops, plundering the towns, and leaving nothing but devastation in their wake. To deal with this situation, God called a farmer named Gideon to lead His people against the Midianites.

When Gideon mustered the men of Israel for battle, thirty-two thousand showed up. Ironically, God told him that was too many! So the Lord had Gideon whittle down his forces to just three hundred men. Backed by the power of God, those three hundred utterly defeated the Midianites and drove them from their land. Through Gideon, God won a great victory on behalf of His people.

I can relate to Gideon, because I grew up in a farming culture. As a boy and as a teen, I worked cotton and cornfields and did a lot of other tasks related to farming. And I sometimes experienced the pain of watching powerful people muscle in and take the fruit of our labors in ways that devastated our family and community. So that legacy probably has a lot to do with why I chose Gideon and his three hundred warriors as a model for what we want to accomplish through R.E.A.L. We're believing God to raise up at least three hundred individuals, churches, businesses, corporations, and/or private foundations who will invest in R.E.A.L.'s vision of connecting economic resources with rural Christian ministries in Mississippi. Ministries like the ones I've described that are breaking the cycle of poverty by bringing the hope of the gospel to young people, helping them realize the value of education, developing Christian leaders in the community, teaching young people skills and habits that will allow them to earn a living, and ultimately creating businesses that provide jobs and the dignity of a paycheck. All in the name of Christ, all motivated by His love.

If reading my story (which is really part of the much greater story of what God is doing in Mississippi) has touched your heart and spoken to your deepest convictions as a follower of Christ, would you consider becoming a member of The 300 Club? Your gift, no matter how big or how small, *will* make a difference.

How do I know? Because as I mentioned in the final chapter, God has taught me never to say *just!* I have every confidence that God will build up the endowment, *just* as He pleases. I set a goal of $5 million, but that's "just" my goal. God knows what He's up to in this beautiful state with its ugly legacy. He is making all things new. And He *will* bring hope to the hopeless and help to the poor, even in rural Mississippi. Imagine the hope and help he will bring to the hopeless and poor in your community as you pray with others, find ways to give of your time, talents, and money, and build bridges so people who don't look like each other can work together as the body of Christ in the name of Jesus and for beautifying the gospel everywhere. *Just* you wait and see!